LEARNING CENTERS: SAINTS

# Learning centers
# Saints

Catherine Stewart, O.P.

TWENTY
THIRD 23rd
PUBLICATIONS
NEW LONDON, CT 06320
WWW.23RDPUBLICATIONS.COM

TWENTY-THIRD PUBLICATIONS

A Division of Bayard

One Montauk Avenue, Suite 200

New London, CT 06320

(860) 437-3012 or (800) 321-0411

www.23rdpublications.com

Copyright ©2013 Catherine Stewart, O.P. All rights reserved.
No part of this publication may be reproduced in any manner
without prior written permission of the publisher.
Write to the Permissions Editor.

ISBN: 978-1-58595-908-2

Library of Congress Control Number: 2012955175

Printed in the U.S.A.

# Introduction

Most of us enjoy stories. We enjoy hearing stories about friends and relatives. Stories teach us lessons we don't even know we are learning. We also enjoy telling stories about our friends or about ourselves.

The stories of the saints contained in this book call us to reflect on the blessings we receive from the lives of these holy men and women. All of the saints laughed, cried, worked, played, believed, doubted, hoped, and despaired—but through it all they "acted with justice, loved tenderly, and walked humbly with their God" (Micah 6:8) in the ordinary everyday events of their lives.

Some of the saint stories deepen our courage and help us find a voice to speak out against injustices. Other stories propel us toward volunteering to help those in need. Still, other saint stories encourage us to take risks or create new paths as we too try to act with justice, to love tenderly, and to walk humbly with God in the ordinary, everyday events of our lives.

This book can be used in several different ways. First of all, at times catechists need to work with small groups of children—what can the other children do while the teacher is working with a small group? The catechist can set up two or three learning stations, and the children who aren't working directly with the catechist can learn about the saints through these independent activities.

Another way to use this book is to set aside a couple of class times. Divide the class into small groups and have the students rotate through the different centers. The catechist can facilitate learning through asking questions and assisting students as they create the different projects.

A third way to use this book is to create an intergenerational evening focused on the saints. Parents, grandparents, aunts, uncles, and parishioners can be invited for a two-hour session focusing on the saints. All of the centers can be set up in advance, and people can rotate through the different centers.

Another possibility is to create a "Saint Museum." Each student prepares a short talk about one of the saints and dresses like that saint. Saints are placed around the room, and when visitors stop in front of the saint, the saint begins talking about him/herself.

Finally, for the students in grades three through six, the catechist can take the saint stories and put them together one after the other to create a readers' theatre for the students. These can be performed for the younger students, parents, or other guests. Readers' theatres are great because the catechist doesn't need props, costumes, etc; only scripts are needed. The story is told using vocal expression.

This book can comfortably be used in a variety of ways, which allows it to meet the diverse needs of both teachers and students. Be creative! Use this book as a springboard to deepen your students' knowledge and love for the saints. May these holy men and women pray for us as our hearts find a home within their stories.

# A Grateful Heart

As I wrote this book, there were many moments where I paused to give thanks for the many people who supported this project.

Rosanne Coffey, the editor of *RTJ's Creative Catechist*, who innocently asked, "Catherine, did you ever consider writing a book?" Rosanne planted the seed and then, much to my delight, as the editor, she watered the seed and helped it grow.

Father Mark Osterhaus, a good friend of mine who often told stories about the saints in his daily homilies and helped us apply their characteristics to our own lives, which deepened my love and appreciation for these holy men and women.

The monks at Saint Bede Abbey in Peru, Illinois, who provided a sacred space that was so essential in the writing and rewriting of this manuscript.

Lindsey Leach and Sarah Sudkamp, two students at Blackburn College, whose computer skills amazed me as they took my brief sketches and created, resized, and flipped numerous templates for the learning centers. Their energy and enthusiasm was catching. One day I walked into the office area and each of them was wearing a bishop miter! Their assistance was invaluable.

Dominican Sisters of Springfield, Illinois, who never know when or where the next creative bubble is going to emerge, but provide the necessary encouragement and resources to help my dreams become realities.

My family, who has always supported and encouraged me in any endeavor I've undertaken. Without realizing it, they give me great material to include in books and articles.

My colleagues at Blackburn College, who provide me with a variety of opportunities to share my creative passion.

Everyone at Twenty-Third Publications, who made this a very positive experience.

# Table of Contents

| | | |
|---|---|---|
| 1 | **Saint John Neumann** (January 5) | 9 |
| 2 | **Saint André Bessette** (January 6) | 16 |
| 3 | **Saint Marianne Cope** (January 23) | 23 |
| 4 | **Saint Angela Merici** (January 27) | 30 |
| 5 | **Saint Scholastica** (February 10) | 36 |
| 6 | **Saint Katharine Drexel** (March 3) | 42 |
| 7 | **Saint Julie Billiart** (April 8) | 48 |
| 8 | **Saint Catherine of Siena** (April 29) | 53 |
| 9 | **Saint Damien Joseph de Veuster** (May 10) | 59 |
| 10 | **Saint Benedict** (July 11) | 65 |
| 11 | **Saint Kateri Tekakwitha** (July 14) | 71 |
| 12 | **Saint Dominic** (August 8) | 76 |
| 13 | **Saint Edith Stein** (August 9) | 82 |
| 14 | **Saint Peter Claver** (September 9) | 89 |
| 15 | **Saint Pio of Pietrelcina** (September 23) | 94 |
| 16 | **Saint Isaac Jogues** (October 19) | 102 |
| 17 | **Saint Frances Xavier Cabrini** (November 13) | 107 |
| 18 | **Saint Rose Philippine Duchesne** (November 18) | 113 |

# Saint John Neumann

*Feastday: January 5*

## CATECHIST'S PAGE FOR GRADES 1-3

**OBJECTIVES**

■ *To help children learn about Saint John Neumann through "Saint John's Story"*

■ *At center one, to learn about bishop symbols by making a wall hanging*

■ *At center two, to teach others about Saint John Neumann by making log cabins*

**MATERIALS**

■ *Red ribbon or construction paper, 2" wide and 18" long*

■ *Pectoral cross, ring, crozier, miter, and pallium template found on page 9*

■ *Tissue box*

■ *Paper*

■ *Pretzels*

■ *Marshmallow cream*

## Saint John Neumann's story

My parents lived in Bohemia and named me John when I was born. I had four sisters and a brother. When I grew up, I wanted to be a priest, but there were too many priests in Bohemia. I left Bohemia and went to America with the hope of becoming a priest.

I finished my studies before I left my homeland and was ordained a priest right after I arrived in America. I was sent to Buffalo, New York, to work with Father Pax, who asked me if I wanted to work in the city or the country. I chose to work in the country. I helped the farmers build log churches and taught them about God. I enjoyed traveling from farm to farm.

I was made Bishop of Philadelphia in 1852. I built 50 churches and began building a cathedral. I also built close to 100 Catholic schools. I wanted children to learn about God as they learned to read and write. People were very surprised when I died at the age of 48. I was the first American man and American bishop to become a saint.

*Saint John Neumann* 9

## CENTER ONE: Bishop Symbols

When Saint John was ordained a bishop, he received five special symbols; today, newly ordained bishops receive the same symbols. The first symbol is the pectoral cross. The cross is worn on a chain close to the bishop's heart. Next, there is the ring. Each bishop chooses what design he wants on his ring. Wearing this reminds the bishop to care for all of the people in his diocese. When the bishop says Mass, he wears a miter. This is a special headdress, which is a sign of victory. The bishop needs to lead others to their victory in heaven. The bishop also carries a crozier to remind everyone that he is like Jesus, the Good Shepherd. Finally, the bishop wears a pallium that is a huge white collar made from lamb's wool embroidered with six black crosses.

### DIRECTIONS

- Cut out one of each bishop symbol.

- Decorate the symbols.

- Glue the symbols on a strip of red ribbon or construction paper. Make a rectangle paper "name plate" and write the name of your bishop. Glue the "name plate" at the top and add the symbols underneath.

- Hang it in your bedroom where you will remember to pray to St. John Neumann, for your bishop, and all bishops.

Then teach the children this song.

### SAINT JOHN NEUMANN
### (TUNE: ARE YOU SLEEPING?)

*Saint John Neumann*
*Saint John Neumann*
*Worked with farmers*
*Worked with farmers*
*He became a bishop*
*He became a bishop*
*Holy Man*
*Holy Man*

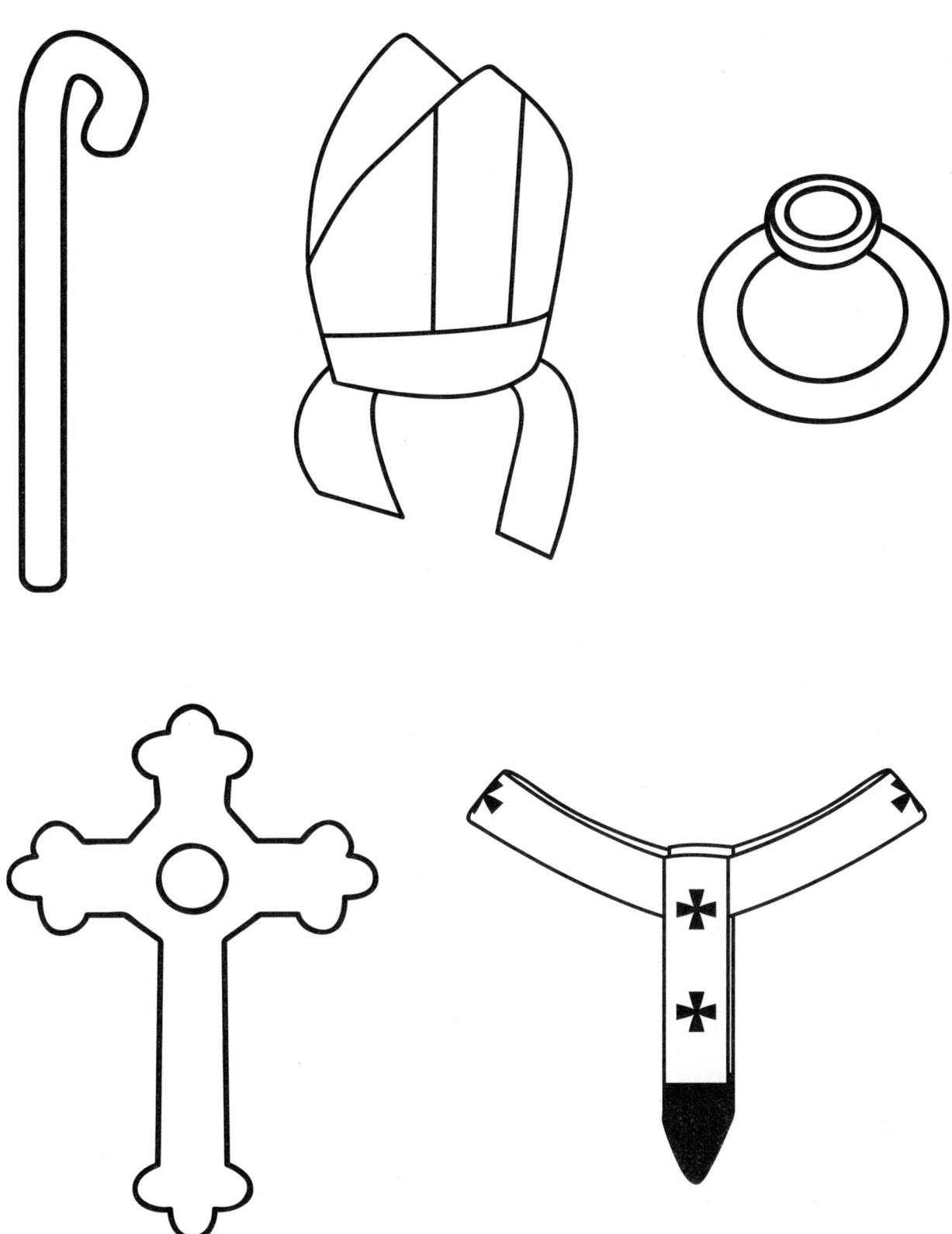

BISHOP SYMBOLS FOR WALL HANGING

*Saint John Neumann*

# Saint John Neumann Cabin

Saint John Neumann lived in a log cabin. Students will remember facts about Saint John Neumann by creating a log cabin.

**DIRECTIONS**

- Get a square tissue box.
- Cut off top.
- Fold paper to make a roof.
- Glue to tissue box.
- Cut out door and windows.
- Use pretzel sticks for the logs and marshmallow cream for the mortar to make a log cabin.
- Write two facts about Saint John Neumann on the cabin.

12 Learning Centers: Saints

# CATECHIST'S PAGE FOR GRADES 4-6

**OBJECTIVES**

■ *To help children learn about Saint John Neumann through "Saint John's Story"*

■ *At center one, to learn the characteristics of a good bishop by making a miter*

■ *At center two, to teach someone else about Saint John Neumann using capes*

**MATERIALS**

■ *Colored paper strips for miter*

■ *Ribbon*

■ *Glue*

■ *Plastic tablecloth*

■ *Markers and pens for writing*

## Saint John Neumann's Story

**READER ONE:** John Neumann was born in Bohemia, a part of the Czech Republic. He studied theology, but he was also interested in botany and astronomy. When he finished studying, he asked to be ordained. The bishop said "No. There are too many priests."

**READER TWO:** John didn't give up his dream, but he boarded a ship and sailed for America. There he was met by Bishop John Dubois who was very excited to ordain him. America had very few priests and needed as many as they could find. He worked with Father Pax in Buffalo, New York. Father Pax asked him if he wanted to work in the city or in the country. Father John chose to work in the country.

**READER THREE:** Father John liked being a priest but he wanted to join the Redemptorist Fathers. Bishop Dubois gave him permission to do this. He traveled from New York to Pittsburgh, Pennsylvania, to become a novice in this order. A few years later, he made his vows.

**READER FOUR:** In 1852, Father John Neumann was appointed as Bishop of Philadelphia. He had many dreams for his diocese. First of all, he established an organized Catholic school system; he built over 200 Catholic schools! That was simply amazing!

**READER FIVE:** Another dream Bishop Neumann had was to have a lot of religious sisters and brothers in his diocese to care for the people.

**READER SIX:** Bishop Neumann was doing errands one day when he collapsed and died. Later, the doctor discovered that he had a stroke. People were very surprised to hear of their bishop's death. He was only 48 years old.

## CENTER ONE

# Bishop Miters

Saint John Neumann received a miter when he was ordained a bishop. Today, bishops also receive miters when they are ordained. The miter symbolizes tongues to represent the fire of the Holy Spirit. Students will focus on the characteristics a man needs in order to be a good bishop, and they will keep these in mind while creating a miter.

**DIRECTIONS**

- Make a bishop's miter.
- Write five characteristics on the miter that a bishop needs. For example: generosity, person of prayer, ability to listen, kindness
- Wear your miter.

**(DIRECTIONS FOR MITER TO GO WITH ILLUSTRATIONS)**

- Take two sheets of paper, and divide them into thirds. Cut on the dotted lines.
- Take another sheet of paper, and draw a heart big enough to cover most of the sheet.
- Cut out the heart. Apply glue to the two humps at the top of the heart (above dotted lines). Secure the heart to the strips you have fit to your head.
- With one of your leftover strips, draw a circle and cut it out.
- Glue the circle to the point of your heart.
- Attach two thick pieces of ribbon to the back of the miter base.
- Draw a cross on your miter and write five bishop characteristics somewhere on it.

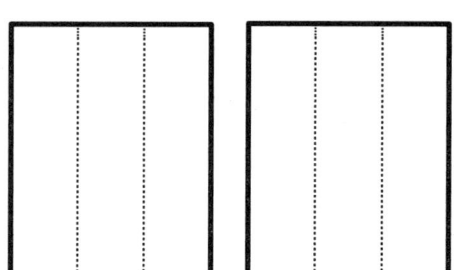
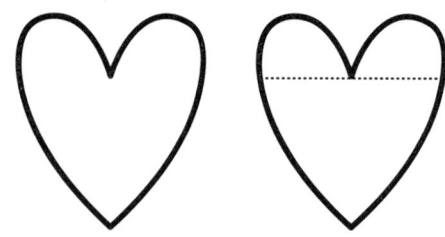

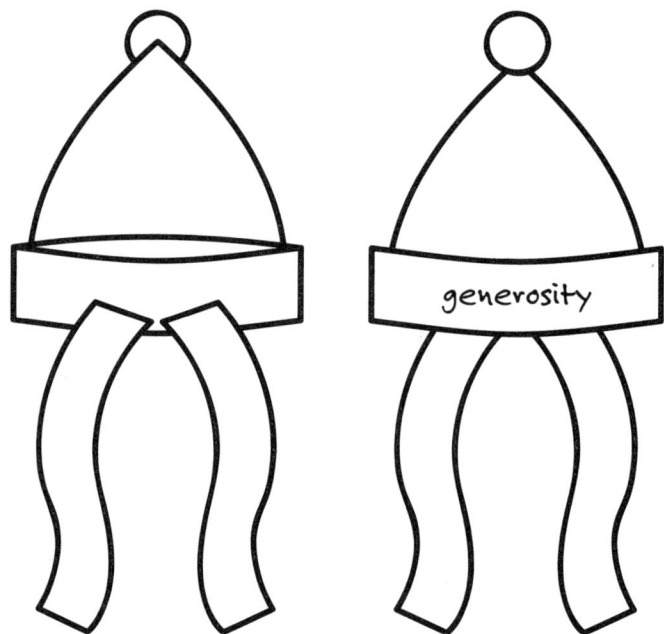

14 Learning Centers: Saints

# Saint John Neumann Capes or Copes

Saint John Neumann wore a cape as a bishop. The cape symbolizes the protection a shepherd gives his sheep. Making a cape will help students remember important facts about Saint John Neumann.

**DIRECTIONS**

- Get a plastic tablecloth. Cut it to desired length.

- Attach 2, 12-inch strips of ribbon to each end to make ties.

- Draw pictures and print words about Saint John Neumann.

- Wear cape.

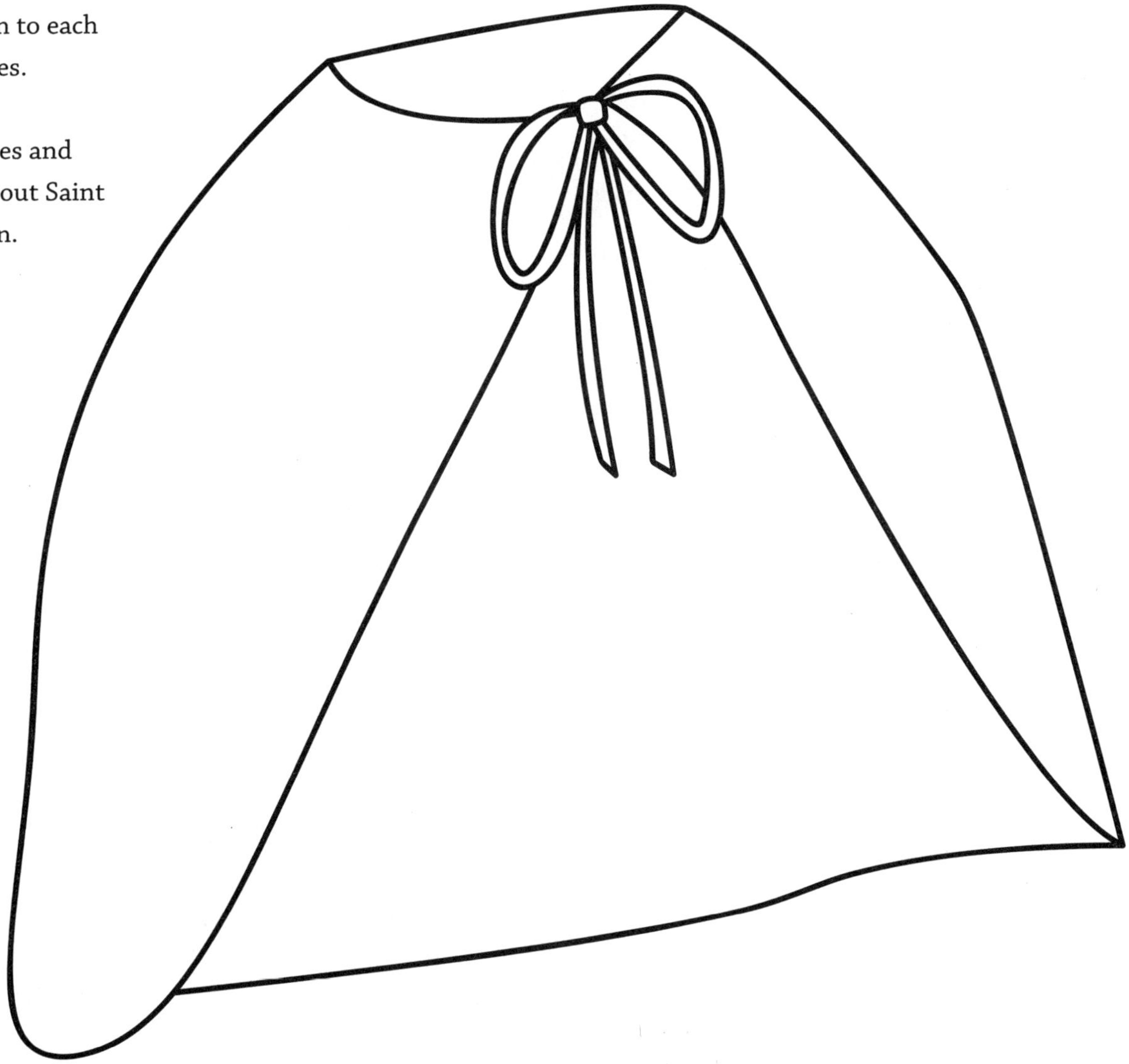

*Saint John Neumann*

# Saint André Bessette

*Feastday: January 6*

## CATECHIST'S PAGE FOR GRADES 1-3

### OBJECTIVES

- *To help children understand Saint André Bessette's life through reading "Saint André's Story"*
- *At center one, to help students understand the prayer of the Anointing of the Sick through designing a stole*
- *At center two, to help students create a memory box for André Bessette.*

### MATERIALS

- *Template of the anointing of the sick symbols for stole*
- *Felt pieces cut into strips of 60" x 5", one per student*
- *Shoe boxes, one per student*
- *Markers/crayons for decorating shoe boxes*
- *Glue*
- *Scissors*

## Saint André's Story

My parents named me Alfred when I was born. Because I was ill, my parents baptized me right away. My family lived in Canada, and we spoke French. My father was a lumberman and was killed by a falling tree. I felt very sad and missed him a lot. My mom took care of us ten children. This was a big job for her. She died three years later, leaving us orphans. I went to live with my aunt and uncle. I tried to do small jobs but I was so sick that I couldn't work, so I spent most of my day praying.

At age 20, I went to live in the United States, where I worked in a factory that made material for clothes. I missed living in Canada. I moved back to Canada and answered God's call to become a religious brother.

I joined The Congregation of the Holy Cross in Canada and received the religious name Brother André.

My main job was to answer the door at Notre Dame College in Quebec. I really enjoyed meeting strangers and helping them. Can you believe I did this for forty years? My favorite saint was Saint Joseph, and I prayed to him every day. Sometimes I would touch a sick person and pray to Saint Joseph and this person would be cured. My dream was to build a special church in honor of Saint Joseph. My dream came true. I died when I was 91 years old. I'm in heaven and enjoy being with God and Saint Joseph.

16 Learning Centers: Saints

# Anointing of the Sick Prayer Stole

Brother André prayed for many people to be healed. Use the dove and praying hands templates to make a prayer stole.

**DIRECTIONS**

■ Make a copy of the prayer sheet for each student. See page 18.

■ Color and decorate the words.

■ Cut out dove and praying hands. Glue them on the stole.

■ Put the stoles on and say the prayer together.

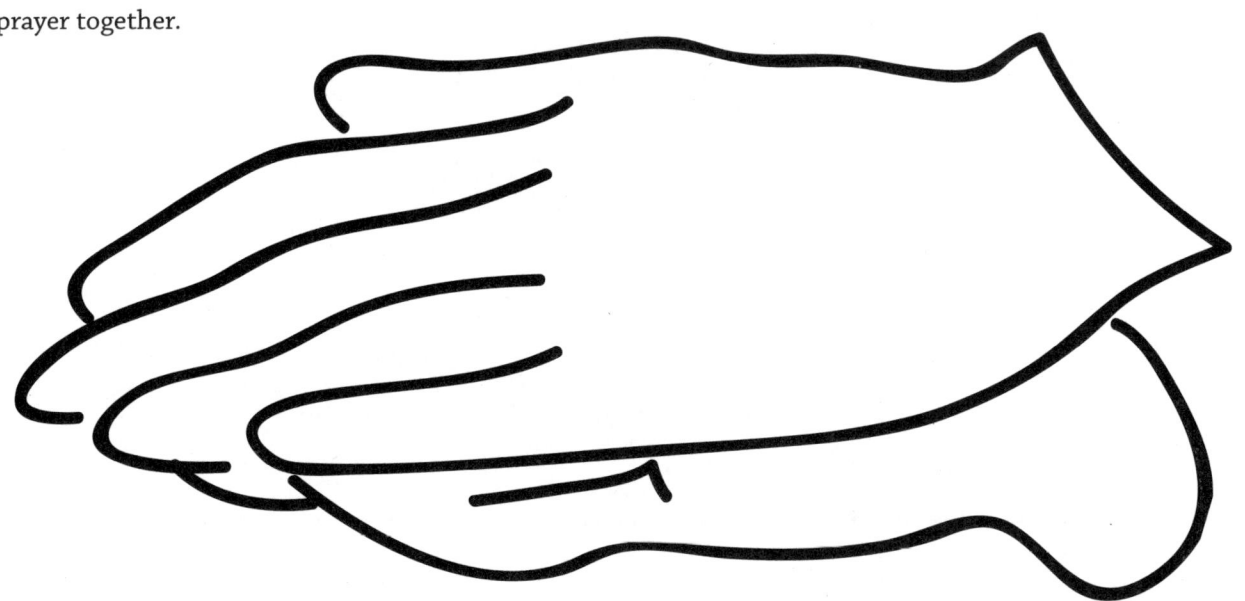

*Saint André Bessette* 17

# Through this holy anointing, may the Lord in his love and mercy help you with the grace of the Holy Spirit

ANOINTING OF THE SICK PRAYER

# Memory Boxes

**CENTER TWO**

Students will show they understand Brother André's life story by making memory boxes. These boxes will help students remember important facts about Brother André.

**DIRECTIONS**

■ Give each student a shoe box to decorate.

■ Print the words "Saint André's memory box" on it.

■ After reading Saint André's story, students can find four to five items to put in André's box that he might have saved. For example, students might put a tree branch inside it to remind them that a tree killed André's father.

*Saint André Bessette*

# CATECHIST'S PAGE FOR GRADES 4-6

## OBJECTIVES

- *To help children understand Saint André Bessette's life through reading "Saint André's Story"*

- *At center one, to help students understand the prayer of the Anointing of the Sick through designing a stole*

- *At center two, to help students create a memory box for André Bessette and write a News Flash about the memory box*

## MATERIALS

- *Template of the anointing of the sick symbols found on page 21.*
- *Felt pieces for stole*
- *Felt stoles, 1 per student*
- *Shoe boxes, one per student*
- *Markers/crayons for decorating shoe boxes*
- *Plain paper for News Flash poster*
- *Glue*
- *Scissors*

## Saint André's Story

**READER ONE:** Alfred Bessette was very weak when he was born. His parents had him baptized immediately. His father was a carpenter and a lumberman, and his mother stayed at home to teach her ten children. His father died when a tree fell on him; his mother was now a single parent of ten children. Three years later, she died. Alfred went to live with his aunt and uncle.

**READER TWO:** Alfred tried to do small jobs to help out, but his health did not let him keep a job. He spent a lot of time praying and talking to his friends about God.

**READER THREE:** When Alfred was 20 years old, he went to the United States to work in a factory that made material for clothes. He worked very hard at this job.

**READER FOUR:** Alfred decided to join the Holy Cross Brothers in Montreal. His religious name was Brother André. His main job was to answer the door at Notre Dame College in Quebec.

**READER FIVE:** Brother André had a special devotion to Saint Joseph. Through Saint Joseph's help, Brother André was often able to heal people. One time when he was scrubbing the floor, two men brought in a lady who could hardly walk. Brother André stopped and prayed and then said to the men, "Let her walk." The woman walked. Brother André wanted people to know it was Saint Joseph who worked the miracles, not him.

**READER SIX:** Brother André had a dream of building a special church to Saint Joseph. With the help of many people, the church was built. Brother André died at the age of 91.

# Anointing of the Sick Prayer Stole

Brother André prayed for many people to be healed. The following prayer is part of the anointing of the sick sacrament; students are introduced to a prayer used throughout the universal church.

**DIRECTIONS**

■ Cut out the words from the prayer template on page 17.

■ Decorate them.

■ Glue them on small pieces of felt.

■ Glue the felt pieces on the stole.

■ Wear your stole sometime during the day and pray for someone who is ill.

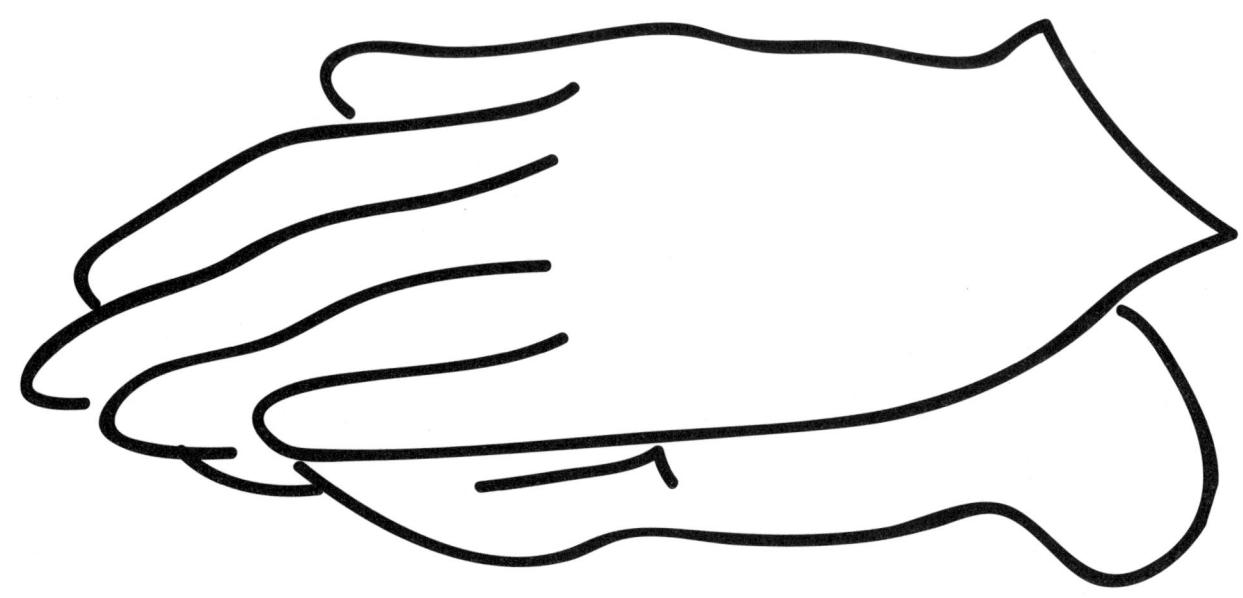

*Saint André Bessette* 21

**CENTER TWO**

# Saint André Memory Boxes and News Flash Posters

Students will show they understand Brother André's life story by making memory boxes; these boxes and posters will help students remember important facts about Brother André.

**DIRECTIONS**

- For the memory box, follow the directions on page 19.

- Design a News Flash Poster about the Memory Box.

22 Learning Centers: Saints

# Saint Marianne Cope

*Feastday: January 23*

---

### CATECHIST'S PAGE FOR GRADES 1-3

---

### OBJECTIVES

■ *To help children understand the life of Saint Marianne Cope through "Saint Marianne's Story"*

■ *At center one, to review the corporal works of mercy through making a charm bracelet*

■ *At center two, to review the important facts of Saint Marianne's life through a Time to Remember clock*

### MATERIALS

■ *Hole punch for charms*
■ *Charm templates*
■ *Yarn for bracelets*
■ *Markers/crayons for decorating charms*
■ *Scissors*
■ *Large paper plates for clocks*
■ *Brads*
■ *Strips of paper ½" by 2"*

## Saint Marianne's Story

I, Maria Anna Barbara Cope, was born in Germany. My family moved to the Unites States when I was one year old. We lived in New York and I went to a Catholic school. My father became ill, so I quit going to school and worked in a factory so my family had money.

After my father died, I became a Franciscan Sister. My new name was Sister Marianne. My job was to teach students. A short time later, I was asked to work in a hospital. I took very good care of the patients.

At that time, there was a very bad disease called leprosy. People who had this disease could not live with their family and friends but had to live on a special island. I was not afraid of the disease so I went to the island to help. I took care of Father Damien, who also helped the lepers. But he caught the disease too. I took care of him until he died. I tried to be a very brave woman. I did not die of leprosy but died of natural causes.

*Saint Marianne Cope* 23

# Corporal Works of Mercy Charm Bracelet

Saint Marianne Cope practiced the corporal works of mercy. Students will be reminded of what these works are as they wear their charm bracelet.

**DIRECTIONS**

■ Choose three different colors of yarn. Braid them together to make a bracelet.

■ Cut out the seven works of mercy charms templates found on page 25, run off on heavy paper.

■ Decorate the charms.

■ Punch a hole in the top of each charm.

■ Put the braided yarn through each hole.

■ Tie the bracelet around your wrist.

## THE CORPORAL WORKS OF MERCY

*To feed the hungry*

*To shelter the homeless*

*To give drink to the thirsty*

*To clothe the naked*

*To visit the imprisoned*

*To visit the sick*

*To bury the dead*

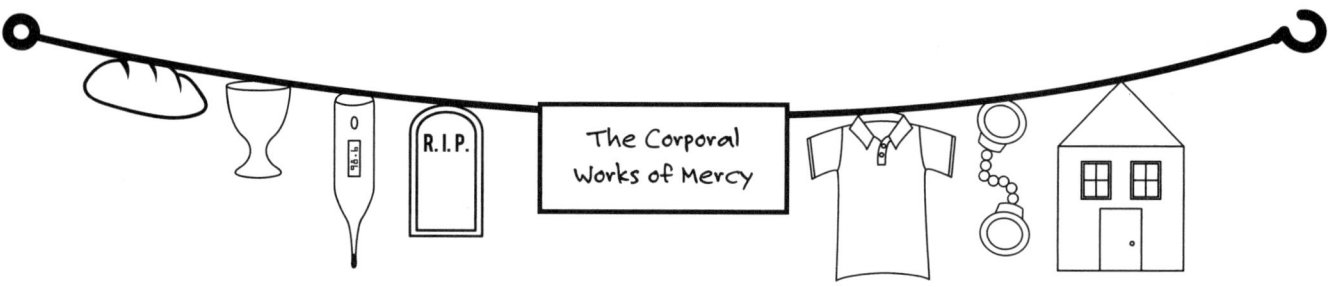

24 Learning Centers: Saints

**CORPORAL WORKS OF MERCY CHARMS**

*Saint Marianne Cope* 25

# Time to Remember

Students will remember important facts about Saint Marianne by making a clock and hanging it in their bedrooms.

**DIRECTIONS**

■ Get a large paper plate.

■ Put lines on it where the numerals would go. Do not put numbers on it.

■ Choose 12 words from Saint Marianne's story that you find interesting.

■ Print one word on each strip.

■ Glue the strips where the numbers would go.

■ Cut out the arrow.

■ Using the brad put the arrow in the center of the plate.

■ Find a friend. Spin the arrow. Tell your friend about the word that the arrow points to.

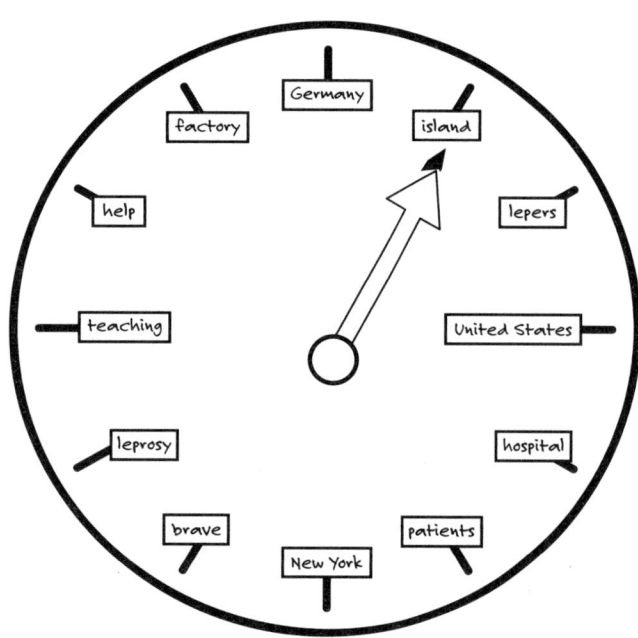

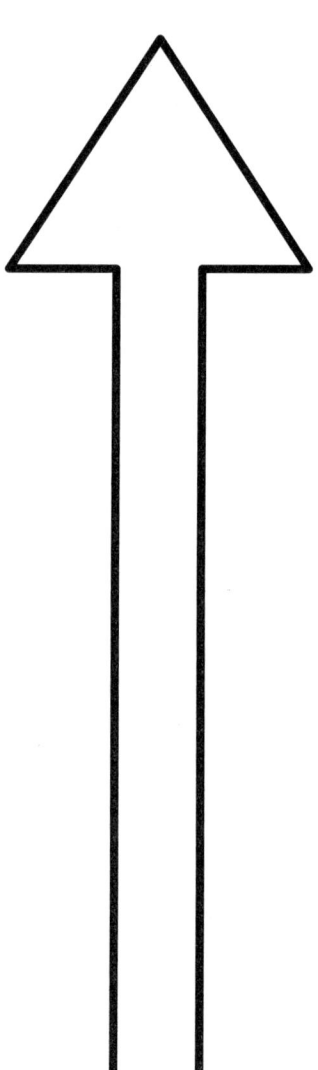

# CATECHIST'S PAGE FOR GRADES 4-6

## OBJECTIVES

- *To help children understand the life of Saint Marianne Cope through "Saint Marianne's Story"*

- *At center one, to review the corporal works of mercy by making symbols on a clothesline*

- *At center two, to review how to care for others by creating the 10 commandments of caring for others*

## MATERIALS

- *Twine for clothesline (15" length for each student)*

- *Small craft clothespins, 7 for each student*

- *Markers/crayons for decorating symbols and commandments*

- *Scissors*

- *10-commandments template found on page 27.*

## Saint Marianne's Story

**READER ONE:** Maria Anna Barbara Cope was born in 1838 in Germany. When Maria was one year old, her family boarded a ship and sailed for America. They made their home in Utica, New York. When she was in 8th grade, her father became very ill. Maria dropped out of school to work in a factory. Her family needed the money she made in order to live.

**READER TWO:** After her father died, her brothers and sisters were old enough to care for themselves. Maria entered the Franciscan order and was given the name Sister Marianne. Sister Marianne taught in schools, and then she was asked to run a hospital.

**READER THREE:** At that time, there was a terribly contagious disease known as leprosy. Once a person got this disease, s/he could no longer live with his/her family. Lepers were sent to live on a special island near Hawaii. Sister Marianne and six sisters went to work on this island. They were not afraid of catching the disease. The sisters knew the lepers needed lots of help.

**READER FOUR:** Father Damien was also helping the lepers. One day, he felt ill, and the doctor told him he had leprosy. Sister Marianne and her sisters not only did their work, but they also took care of Father Damien's work. No one wanted to take care of Father Damien, so Sister Marianne nursed him until he died.

**READER FIVE:** After Father Damien died, Sister Marianne was responsible for his work as well as her own work. Sister Marianne knew she needed assistance. So she looked for a religious community to take Father Damien's work, and she was able to find one. Sister Marianne stayed on the island until she died. She died of natural causes.

# Corporal Works of Mercy Clothesline

## DIRECTIONS

- Get a sheet of paper with the corporal works of mercy symbols.

- Decorate with markers/crayons.

- Draw a symbol for each corporal work of mercy and write the corporal work of mercy on the back.

- Take a small rectangle piece of paper and write "The Corporal Works of Mercy" to hang on the clothesline.

- Get a piece of twine and clothespins.

- Hang the symbols on the twine.

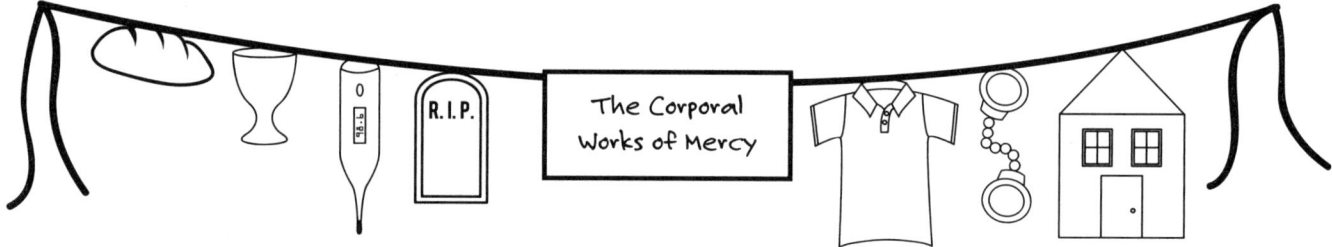

# Care for Others Commandments

Sister Marianne cared for everyone; students are encouraged to follow her example through writing the commandments of care and posting them in their bedrooms.

## DIRECTIONS

- Think of ten rules that would help everyone care for all people.

- Write them on the Ten commandment template.

- Decorate.

- Share with your class.

# CARING FOR OTHERS COMMANDMENTS

# Saint Angela Merici

*Feastday: January 27*

---

### CATECHIST'S PAGE FOR GRADES 1-3

---

**OBJECTIVES**

■ *To learn about Saint Angela's life through "Saint Angela's Story"*

■ *At center one, to learn the fruits of the Spirit through making apple prints*

■ *At center two, to practice making good choices through Just Say No posters*

**MATERIALS**

■ *Red, yellow, and green tempera paint*

■ *Apples cut in half*

■ *12" x 18" sheets of paper for apple stamps*

■ *11"x 14" sheets of paper for NO poster*

■ *Markers/pens*

■ *Large letters NO*

## Saint Angela's Story

A big sister welcomed me home when I was born. She loved my name: Angela. We grew up in France, and when I was 10 years old, my parents died. My sister and I felt very sad; we went to live with our uncle, who was very kind to us. My sister died suddenly. I cried and cried. One night, I dreamed that I saw my sister in heaven with all the saints; this made me very happy.

At this time, only boys went to school. Girls stayed home to learn how to cook and clean. I believed girls needed to go to school too, so I turned my home into a school and taught girls.

One day while I was praying, I had a vision that showed me that I was to gather women together and build schools for girls. I talked to the pope about my dream and he asked me to found an order for nursing sisters. I told the pope "No," because I knew God wanted me to educate young women. I felt very scared when I told the pope "No." I knew I had to do what God wanted.

I gathered 12 women together and we became known as the Company of Saint Ursula. We began educating all young women; before this, only rich women and nuns were tutored. It was hard work, but the girls were so happy to learn. We became the first teaching order of nuns in the world. All of the other Sisters spent their time in a cloister (a special place where nuns live) praying. I was happy when I died, because I did what God asked me to do.

---

30 Learning Centers: Saints

**CENTER ONE**

# Fruits of the Spirit Apple Prints

**DIRECTIONS**

■ Get a large piece of paper.

■ At the top of the paper print "Fruits of the Spirit."

■ Get an apple slice for stamping.

■ Dip the cut apple into the paint.

■ "Stamp" the apple onto the paper.

■ Do this 9 times, using a variety of paint colors.

■ Let dry.

■ Write one of the fruits of the Spirit on each apple.

■ The fruits of the Spirit are love, joy, peace, patience, kindness, goodness, faithfulness, self-control, and gentleness.

■ Color in the background.

*Saint Angela Merici*

## CENTER TWO: Just Say No Poster

**DIRECTIONS**

■ Make a poster with the words as shown.

■ Write words or phrases inside each letter that remind you to "Say No."

■ Decorate the page.

For example:
- *Disobeying*
- *Fighting with my brother or sister*
- *Whining*

# CATECHIST'S PAGE FOR GRADES 4-6

**OBJECTIVES**

■ *To learn about Saint Angela's life through "Saint Angela's Story"*

■ *At center one, to learn the fruits of the Spirit by making an apple slice ribbon hanging*

■ *At center two, to practice making good choices by making a poster and writing a skit*

**MATERIALS**

■ *Red, yellow, and green tempera paint*

■ *Apples cut in half*

■ *12" x 18" sheets of paper for "apple stamps"*

■ *11" x 14" sheets of paper for "NO" poster*

■ *Markers/pens*

■ *Grades 4-6 also need scissors and 1"- wide ribbon (cut in 15" lengths)*

## Saint Angela's Story

**READER ONE:** Angela was born in France and had an older sister. When Angela was 10 years old, her parents died; she and her sister went to live with their uncle. Her sister died suddenly. Angela was very sad. One night she dreamed she saw her sister in heaven with all the saints; this made Angela happy. Her uncle died when she was 20.

**READER TWO:** At this time, only boys went to school. Girls stayed home to learn how to cook, clean, and sew. Angela believed girls needed to go to school to learn too. Angela taught girls in her home, which she turned into a school. Angela had a vision that showed her that she was to gather women together to carry out the mission of teaching girls in schools. The pope asked Angela to found an order for nursing sisters. Angela told the pope "No," because she knew God wanted her to educate young women.

**READER THREE:** Angela gathered 12 women together, and they became known as the Company of Saint Ursula. They began educating all young women; before this, only rich women and nuns were tutored. In those days, women were not allowed to teach, nor were they allowed to go anywhere alone. Religious sisters had to stay in their cloister and pray.

**READER FOUR:** There were not any teaching sisters as there are today. Angela's dream of creating a teaching order was very special. Angela founded the first teaching order of women. Because Angela's dream was so different, people often made fun of her and her sisters. Angela knew she was doing what God wanted and continued to do it even though it was difficult. Angela died in 1540.

*Saint Angela Merici*

# Fruits of the Spirit Apple Prints

**CENTER ONE**

**DIRECTIONS**

- Get a large piece of paper, scissors, and piece of string or ribbon.

- Get an apple slice.

- Dip the cut apple into the paint.

- "Stamp" the apple onto the paper.

- Do this 9 times, using a variety of paint colors.

- Let dry.

- Print one of the fruits of the Spirit on each apple.

- The fruits of the Spirit are love, joy, peace, patience, kindness, goodness, faithfulness, self-control, and gentleness.

- Cut out the fruits of the Spirit, and on the back of each one write a way that you can practice that fruit of the Spirit.

- Using clear tape, attach each one on the ribbon, leaving room at the top to tie a loop for hanging.

## CENTER TWO: Just Say No Poster and Skit

**DIRECTIONS**

■ Make a Just Say No poster. See page 32.

■ Find a friend and create a skit using your Just Say No poster. Perform it for another group of friends.

For example:

*Disobeying*

*Cheating on a test*

*Lying*

*Saint Angela Merici*

# Saint Scholastica

*Feastday: February 10*

### CATECHIST'S PAGE FOR GRADES 1-3

### OBJECTIVES

- To help children understand the life of Saint Scholastica through reading the "Saint Scholastica's Story"
- At center one, to keep the beat with a rain stick while singing a song about Saint Scholastica
- At center two, read *The Holy Twins* by Kathleen Norris and Tomie dePaola; design a paper quilt with favorite scenes.

### MATERIALS

- *Paper towel rolls for making rain sticks, one per student*
- *Rice*
- *Cupcake papers, 2 per student*
- *Glue*
- *Markers for decorating rain sticks*
- *The Holy Twins by Kathleen Norris and Tomie dePaola*
- *Quilt block template, nine for each student*
- *Large sheet of paper for gluing templates onto*
- *Variety of strips of ribbon for quilt*

## Saint Scholastica's Story

Do you like thunderstorms? Did you ever pray for one? I did! Saint Benedict and I were twins. We liked to play together. When we grew up, we both entered religious orders. We only saw each other once a year.

We spent a lot of time talking about God and praying together. One time Benedict told me that it was time for him to go back to the monastery. I did not want him to leave, and I prayed for a thunderstorm. It rained so hard that Benedict could not leave. He was angry with me. But Benedict forgave me and stayed the night and talked with me.

Three days later, while Benedict was praying, he had a vision in which he saw my soul leave my body in the form of a dove. He sent some of his religious brothers to my convent, and they found me dead just as Benedict said. They wrapped up my body and brought it back to the monastery. They buried me in a tomb.

36 Learning Centers: Saints

# Rain Sticks

**CENTER ONE**

Saint Scholastica prayed for rain so her brother would stay and visit longer. Students will remember this story by making rain sticks.

**DIRECTIONS**

■ Decorate the paper towel roll. Use markers or paints or tissue paper dipped in glue and water.

■ Let it dry.

■ Take one cupcake paper and glue it to one end of the paper towel roll.

■ Put in some rice. Shake it back and forth, if you like the sound, glue the other cup cake paper on the other end.

■ If you don't like the sound, add more rice until you do, then glue the cupcake paper on the other end.

■ Keep the beat while singing the following song:

### SCHOLASTICA (TUNE: ARE YOU SLEEPING?)

*Saint Scholastica,*
*Saint Scholastica*
*Holy Twin,*
*Holy Twin*
*Prayed for a big thunderstorm*
*Prayed for a big thunderstorm*
*Saint Scholastica*
*Saint Scholastica*

*Saint Scholastica*

# Paper Quilt

Students will remember facts about Saint Scholastica and Saint Benedict through making a quilt based on their favorite parts of the book, *The Holy Twins*.

**DIRECTIONS**

- Read *The Holy Twins*.

- Using the quilt block template, draw nine favorite parts of the story.

- Glue your blocks in three rows of three on a large sheet of paper.

- Put strips of ribbon in between.

- Share with a friend.

# CATECHIST'S PAGE FOR GRADES 4-6

## OBJECTIVES

■ *To help children understand the life of Saint Scholastica through reading the "Story of Saint Scholastica"*

■ *At center one, create a rap about Saint Scholastica; use the rain stick to help keep the rhythm*

■ *At center two, read* The Holy Twins *by Kathleen Norris and Tomie dePaola; make a pop-up book using two scenes from Saint Scholastica's life.*

## MATERIALS

■ *Paper towel rolls for making rain sticks, one per student*

■ *Rice for rain sticks*

■ *Cupcake papers, 2 per student*

■ *Glue*

■ *Markers for decorating rain sticks*

■ *The Holy Twins by Kathleen Norris and Tomie dePaola*

■ *Paper for making pop-up books*

## Saint Scholastica's Story

**READER ONE:** Do you like thunderstorms? Did you ever pray for a thunderstorm? This saint did! Scholastica was the twin sister of Saint Benedict; they were very close.

**READER TWO:** Scholastica became a sister of a religious order. Every year Benedict and Scholastica met in a house; they spent the day praying together and talking of God. It was growing late in the afternoon, so Benedict and Scholastica sat down to share a meal. It began to grow dark and Benedict prepared to leave. She said, "Benedict, stay the night so we can talk until morning about the joys of heaven."

**READER THREE:** Benedict was very surprised by Scholastica's request. He replied, "What? Scholastica you know I cannot stay away from the monastery. I need to get back; I can't break the rules." Scholastica quietly folded her arms on the table and placed her head on her arms and began to pray. When she raised her head, there was a huge clap of thunder, a bolt of lightning, and rain that pounded the earth. It rained so hard that Benedict could not leave the house and return to his monastery.

**READER FOUR:** Benedict was very angry with his sister. He said, "May God have mercy on you, sister. Why did you do this?" Scholastica answered, "See, I asked you and you would not listen to me. So, I asked God, and he listened to me. Leave me and return to the monastery." Benedict stayed, and the two of them talked about God and God's many blessings. After it stopped raining, Benedict returned to the monastery.

**READER FIVE:** Perhaps Scholastica knew this was their last visit. Three days later, Benedict was standing in his room and had a vision of Scholastica's soul leaving her body and rising up to heaven in the form of a dove. He sent several monks to the convent; they found Scholastica dead just as Benedict said. They wrapped up her body and brought it to the monastery, where it was placed in a tomb.

# Rain Sticks

Saint Scholastica prayed for rain so her brother would stay and visit longer. Students will remember this story by making rain sticks.

**DIRECTIONS**

■ Make the rain sticks according to the directions on page 37.

■ Create a rap about Saint Scholastica.

■ Perform your rap for your friends. Be sure to use your rain sticks.

*Here's a sample Scholastica Rap*

**Scholastica and Benedict were twins**

**Silence and solitude were in**

**Once a year they visited and shared**

**It was easy to see their love and care**

**Benedict wanted to leave and Scholastica wanted him to stay**

**She prayed for rain today**

**It rained so hard, that stay he did**

**Together they talked until the moon hid**

# Pop-Up Scenes

Students will remember facts about Saint Scholastica and Saint Benedict after reading *The Holy Twins* and making a pop-up book with their two favorite scenes. Be sure to share with a friend.

**DIRECTIONS**

- Take a sheet of paper and fold it in half.

- Cut two slits along the fold.

- Open up your sheet of paper and push the slit of paper up, making a step.

- Draw your scene, cut it out, and glue it to the step on your book.

*Saint Scholastica* 41

# Saint Katharine Drexel

*Feastday: March 3*

## CATECHIST'S PAGE FOR GRADES 1-3

### OBJECTIVES

■ To help children understand the life of Sister Katharine Drexel by reading "Saint Katharine's Story"

■ At center one, help the children understand that "Eucharist" means "thanksgiving," by creating a cornucopia

■ At center two, help the children understand that everyone is called to help others, by making a vocation drum

### MATERIALS

■ *Brown paper for making cornucopia, one piece for each student*

■ *Markers for writing*

■ *1 potato chip can with both ends removed for each student*

■ *2 large balloons for each student*

■ *2 heavy rubber bands for each student*

## Saint Katharine's Story

My older sister, Elizabeth, was so excited when I was born because she would have someone to play with. My mother died when I was a baby. My dad felt sad; we went to live with relatives. Our father remarried, and our stepmother was very kind to us. Our family had lots of money, and we shared it with the poor.

Every week our family went to church, and every evening we prayed together.

Elizabeth and I were so excited when our stepsister was born. The three of us were very good friends.

One time, our family went on vacation out west. I saw how poor the Native Americans were on their reservation, and I decided I would help them when I grew up.

When my father died, he left me a lot of money. A bishop wrote to me and told me about his dream of building a school for the Native Americans. I founded a religious order of sisters that focused on Jesus as well as on helping the Native Americans. We built several schools for the Native Americans. I was very happy; I helped people understand the Native Americans were just as important as everyone else.

I died at the age of 96. I went to heaven knowing that I helped others know that God's love was big enough for everyone.

# Eucharistic Cornucopias

**CENTER ONE**

Saint Katharine received the Eucharist every week. Eucharist means "thanksgiving." Students will be aware of the many gifts for which they are thankful by making this cornucopia.

**DIRECTIONS**

- Roll the paper to make a cornucopia.

- On the outside, print the letters E U C H A R I S T as shown.

- Next to each letter, print a word that starts with that letter for which you are grateful.

- Take your cornucopia home and put it in the center of your table.

- Fill it with fruits and vegetables.

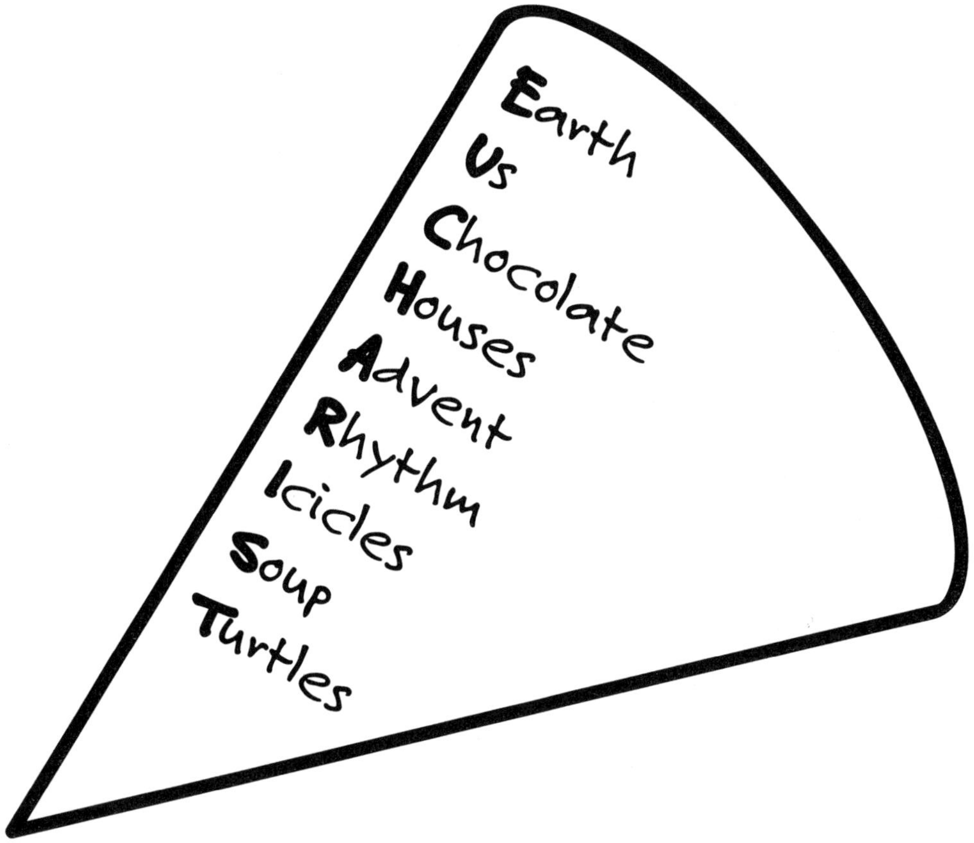

*Earth*
*Us*
*Chocolate*
*Houses*
*Advent*
*Rhythm*
*Icicles*
*Soup*
*Turtles*

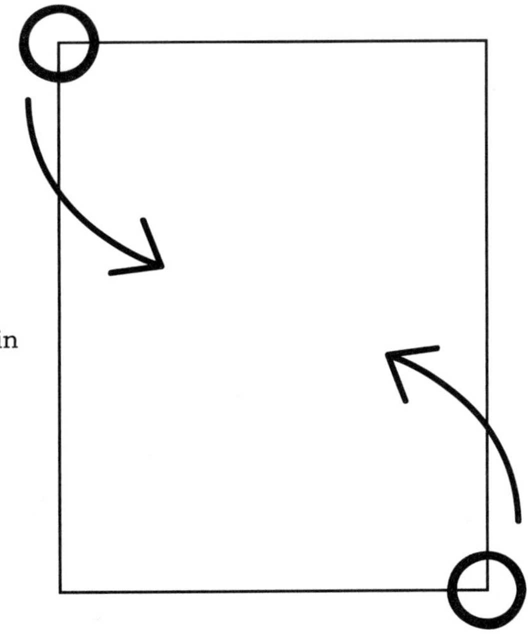

To fold your cornucopia, take opposite ends of the paper and meet them. Begin rolling into a cone shape, and use tape to secure.

*Saint Katharine Drexel* 43

**CENTER TWO**

# Vocation Drums

Saint Katharine worked with the Native Americans. The Native Americans used drums to praise God. You too can praise God by doing acts of kindness. This drum will help you remember to do an act of kindness.

**DIRECTIONS**

■ Take the potato chip can.

■ Cut the open end off the large balloon.

■ Stretch the closed end of the balloon over one end of the potato chip can. Hold the balloon in place with a heavy rubber band and smooth out all the wrinkles to make it very tight.

■ Do the same thing on the other end.

■ God calls every person to help others. We need to tell God that we are willing to do this.

■ Very carefully on the side of the drum print the following: "I will help one person every day."

■ Play your drum.

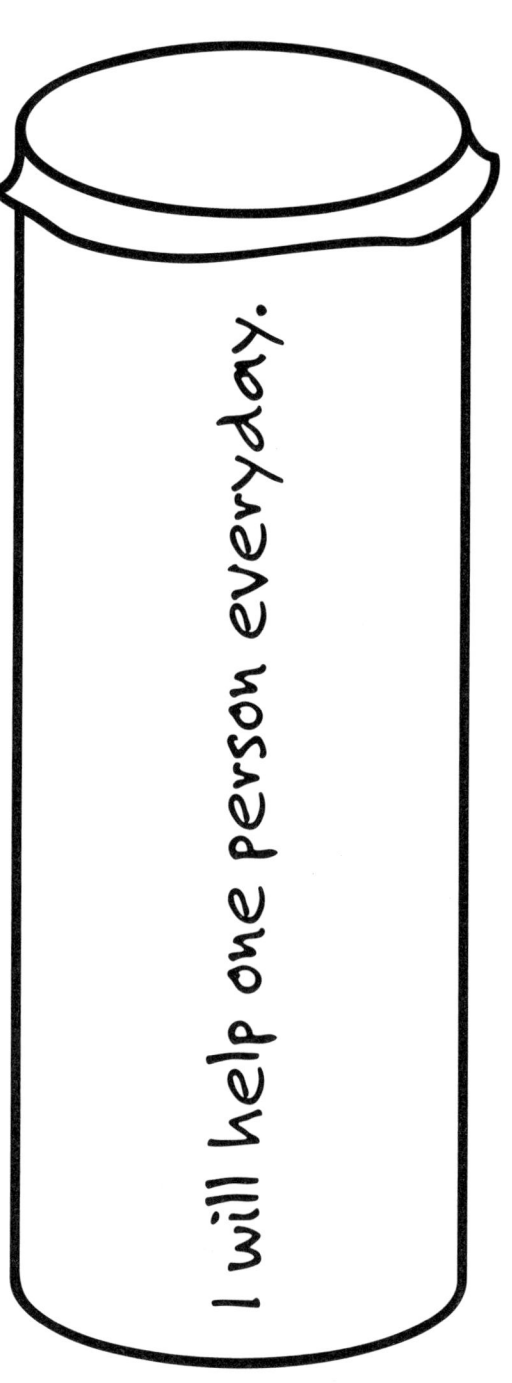

# CATECHIST'S PAGE FOR GRADES 4-6

**OBJECTIVES**

- *To help children understand the life of Sister Katharine Drexel by reading "Saint Katharine's Story"*

- *At center one, help the children understand they are missionaries every day by making missionary motto boards*

- *At center two, help the children understand that everyone can be viewed from two perspectives, by making perspective posters*

**MATERIALS**

- *Thick yarn or string for sandwich boards*

- *Markers for writing missionary mottos and making perspective posters*

- *2 pieces of poster board for each student*

- *2 pieces of paper, 8½" x 11" for each student*

## Saint Katharine's Story

**READER ONE:** Katharine Drexel was born in Philadelphia. Katharine's mother died when she was a baby. Eventually, her father remarried. Their family was very wealthy and gave a lot of money to hospitals, schools, orphanages, and homes for the elderly to help the poor. Elizabeth and Katharine welcomed Louise, their stepsister, into their family.

**READER TWO:** Katharine watched her stepmother help the poor, and she wanted to help them too. Her family took a trip out west, and Katharine saw how poor the Native American were.

Francis Drexel died in 1885. Francis left the girls 14 million dollars. Katharine received a visit from the bishop who served the Indians in the Dakota Territory, and from Father Stephan, who worked with the Catholic Indian Bureau. Both men talked about the needs of the Native Americans on the Rosebud Reservation. Katharine decided to give money to them.

**READER THREE:** While in Europe, Katharine received letters from Bishop Marty describing his dream to build a school for the Native American children. Katharine visited several monasteries asking for either money or missionaries to support the Native American Reservation and was told "no." She went to the pope and requested his help, and he replied, "Why not, my child, yourself become a missionary?"

**READER FOUR:** The three sisters traveled out west to visit the Native American Reservation. They realized that the Natives did not just need money, but they needed people to minister to them. In 1891, Katharine founded The Sisters of the Blessed Sacrament. The sisters founded many schools and helped the Native Americans.

**READER FIVE:** Sister Katharine died on March 3, 1955, at the age of 96. Mother Katharine could rest in peace knowing she helped others know that God's love was big enough for everyone.

### CENTER ONE

# Missionary Mottos

Saint Katharine was a missionary; she taught others about God. We are called to teach others about God through words and example. The sandwich board will help students choose ways they can share the Good News.

**DIRECTIONS**

- Get two pieces of poster board.

- Punch holes in the top of each piece.

- Using thick yarn or heavy string, tie them together to make a sandwich board.

- On one side write your name.

- Decorate with pictures that describe who you are.

- On the other board, write the word "Missionaries," vertically.

- Describe how you will be a missionary to those you meet each day.

46 Learning Centers: Saints

**CENTER TWO**

# Perspective Posters

Saint Katharine had many gifts. Sometimes our gifts are also the reasons why people don't accept us. These posters will help students understand that a gift can be viewed from a different perspective and be seen as a limitation. For example, some people would view Saint Katharine has a heroine because she gave money to the poor; others would view her as a "criminal" because she was always asking people for money and helping minorities.

**DIRECTIONS**

- Design a Heroine Poster on a piece of paper for Sister Katharine Drexel.
- Draw a picture of Sister Katharine Drexel.
- Write sentences under her picture that describe why she is a hero.
- Design a Wanted Poster on the other paper for Sister Katharine Drexel.
- Draw her picture and write sentences that describe why some people might see her as a criminal.

*Saint Katharine Drexel* 47

# Saint Julie Billiart

*Feastday: April 8*

---

**CATECHIST'S PAGE FOR GRADES 1-3**

---

### OBJECTIVES

■ To learn about Saint Julie through "Saint Julie's Story"

■ At center one, to learn the symbols of the four gospel writers

■ At center two, to review the parable of the Good Samaritan and become aware of the many acts of kindness performed each day

### MATERIALS

■ Large drinking straws, 2 per student

■ Gospel writers' symbols template on page 49

■ Yarn for hanging mobile

■ Markers/crayons for decorating

■ Glue

■ Magic glasses template

## Saint Julie's Story

I was born in 1751 in Cuvilly, France. My parents named me Julie. I was the fifth of seven children. I loved to play school, and I was very smart. Most children made their First Communion at the age of 13; however, my pastor knew I had a special relationship with God, and he let me make my First Communion when I was nine years old. This was a very special day for me, one that I never forgot!

I became a teacher when I grew up. At recess time, I often sat on a haystack and taught my friends the parables from the Bible. One of my favorite stories was the Good Samaritan.

When I was 22 years old, a terrible thing happened to my father. Someone tried to kill him, and I was so scared, the shock made my legs paralyzed for 22 years. While I was paralyzed, I prayed a lot. One day I had a vision in which I saw a group of sisters dressed in habits I never saw before; God called me to found a religious order, the Sisters of Notre Dame de Namur.

Our main ministry was teaching. The year after I founded the order, I was once again able to walk. My life was filled with happy and sad moments. I died when I was 64 years old.

---

48  Learning Centers: Saints

# Gospel Writers' Symbols Mobile

**CENTER ONE**

Saint Julie taught her friends parables that are found in the four gospels. Students will learn the symbols for the four gospel writers by making a mobile.

### DIRECTIONS

- Create the four-sided mobile by gluing two straws together to form an "X".
- Cut out the four symbols and decorate.
- Punch a hole in the top of each symbol.
- Hang onto the mobile.

**Matthew**

**Mark**

**Luke**

**John**

*Saint Julie Billiart* 49

# Magic Glasses

**CENTER TWO**

Saint Julie encouraged her students to help others. By wearing these glasses, students will become more aware of people they can help.

- Read the parable of the Good Samaritan.

- Talk about how the Samaritan was a friend to the man who was hurt.

- Cut out your magic glasses.

- Wear your magic glasses and look for people doing nice things for other people.

**DIRECTIONS FOR MAGIC GLASSES:**

- Cut out the templates.

- Cut the middles out of glasses to make room for your eyes.

- Tape or glue the earpieces to your glasses.

- Decorate your glasses.

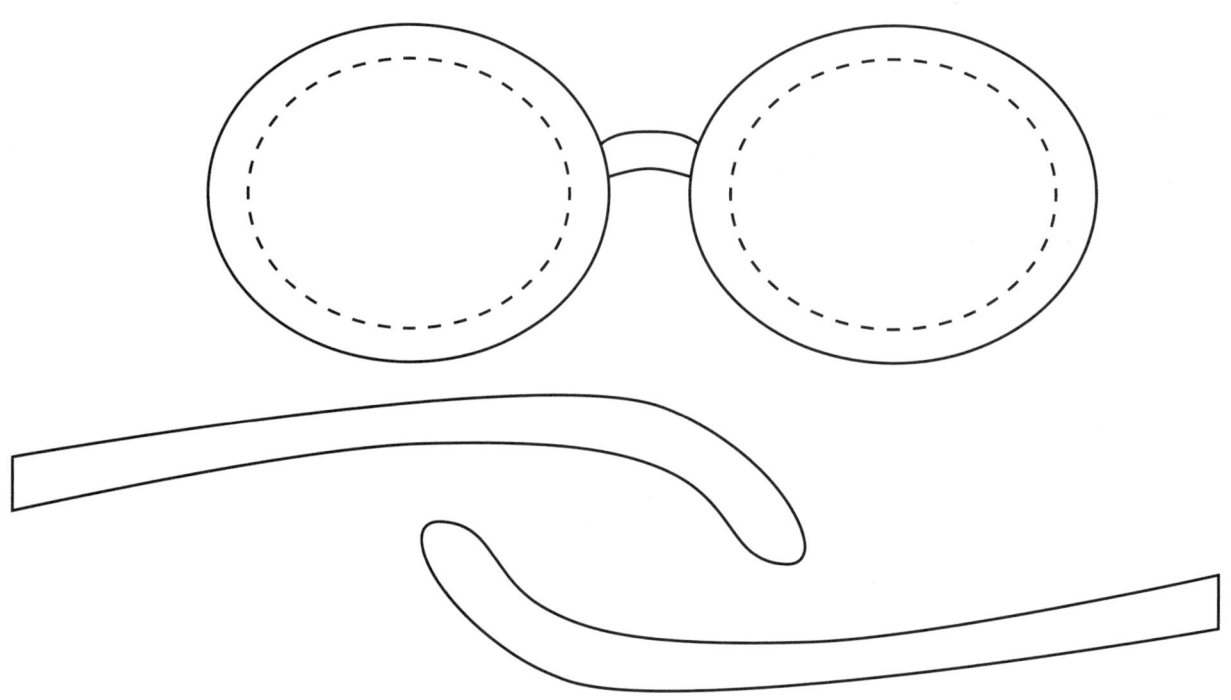

50 Learning Centers: Saints

# CATECHIST'S PAGE FOR GRADES 4-6

**OBJECTIVES**

- *To learn about Saint Julie through "Saint Julie's Story"*
- *At center one, to learn the symbols of the four gospel writers by making a mobile*
- *At center two, to review the parable of the Good Samaritan, by creating a Glogster poster of random acts of kindness*

**MATERIALS**

- *Paper for making a four-sided mobile*
- *Template of gospel writers' symbols*
- *Yarn for hanging mobile*
- *Markers/crayons for decorating*
- *Glue*
- *Parable of the Good Samaritan*

## Saint Julie's Story

**READER ONE:** Julie Billiart was born in Cuvilly, France, in 1751. Julie was the fifth of seven children. She loved to play school, and she was very smart. At this time, most children made their First Communion at the age of 13; however, Julie's pastor knew she had a special relationship with God, and he allowed her to make her First Communion when she was nine.

**READER TWO:** When Julie was 16, she became a teacher. At recess time, she often sat on a haystack and taught her friends the parables from the Bible. Teaching was a life-long career for Julie.

**READER THREE:** When Julie was 22 years old, someone tried to kill her father. This scared Julie so much that her legs were paralyzed for 22 years. During this time, she prayed a lot.

**READER FOUR:** When the French Revolution broke out; Julie hid priests in her home to protect them from being killed. She had to move five different times in order to save her own life.

**READER FIVE:** Julie had a vision in which she saw a group of sisters dressed in a habit she never saw before. God called her to found a religious order, the Sisters of Notre Dame de Namur. Their main mission was to teach.

**READER SIX:** Julie was elected as the leader of the young group of sisters. The year after Julie founded the order, she was once again able to walk. Julie's life was filled with happy and sad moments. She died on April 8, 1816, at the age of 64.

*Saint Julie Billiart*

 **CENTER ONE**

# Gospel Writers' Symbols Mobile

Saint Julie taught her friends parables that are found in the four gospels. Students will learn the symbols for the four gospel writers by making this mobile.

**DIRECTIONS**

■ Follow the same directions for the mobile as on page 49.

**CENTER TWO**

# Glogster Poster: Random Acts of Kindness

Saint Julie Billiart was known for her acts of kindness, which means we could also say she was a Good Samaritan. Looking for acts of kindness in our lives will help us act more like Saint Julie.

**DIRECTIONS**

■ Read the parable of the Good Samaritan (Luke 10:25-37)

■ Throughout the day, see if you can catch others being kind.

■ Go to www.edu.glogster.com and create a poster using phrases and pictures to show random acts of kindness.

■ Create an account.

■ Click on *Poster Yourself*

■ Choose *Classic Glog*

■ Begin Creating! (Choose backgrounds, text boxes, and more!)

52 Learning Centers: Saints

# 8

# Saint Catherine of Siena

*Feastday: April 29*

**CATECHIST PAGE FOR GRADES 1-3**

### OBJECTIVES

■ *To help children learn about Saint Catherine of Siena through reading "Saint Catherine's Story"*

■ *At center one, learn the four types of prayer through making a standing cube*

■ *At center two, review facts about Saint Catherine through writing a haiku*

### MATERIALS

■ *Variety of 8 ½" x11" colored paper for making standing cubes, 2 sheets for each student*

■ *Variety of magazines for cutting out pictures*

■ *Scissors*

■ *Glue*

■ *Markers for writing*

■ *Watercolors/brushes, enough for your class*

■ *Watercolor paper, one sheet per student*

## Saint Catherine's Story

Can you imagine being the youngest of 25 children? Think how many older brothers and sisters you would have to "boss" you around!

I was born in northern Italy, in a city called Siena in 1847. I was the youngest of 25 children. When I was little, I saw Jesus, who smiled at me and blessed me.

When I grew up, my parents wanted me to get married, but I wanted to be a nun. I joined the Third Order of Dominican Sisters, which were a group of laymen and laywomen. I wore the black and white habit. I spent a lot of time by myself in silence. I prayed for everyone in the world.

One night when I was praying, Jesus and the Blessed Mother appeared to me. Jesus gave me a ring. This was a symbol that Jesus and I were very special to each other. Jesus also told me to spend more time helping people and less time praying. So I began to give food to the poor, and take the sick to the hospital. Many people saw my kindness, and joined me in helping others.

At the time I lived, there was much fighting in the world. I wrote letters to kings and queens to ask them to stop the fighting. I died when I was 33 years old. I did my best to do what God wanted me to do and worked hard to bring peace to the world.

*Saint Catherine of Siena* 53

# Prayer Cubes

**CENTER ONE**

Saint Catherine used the four types of prayer every day (thanksgiving, petition, praise, and contrition). Students will learn and remember these types of prayer through making a prayer cube.

**DIRECTIONS**

■ Make a cube.

■ On plain paper, print the words: Thanksgiving, Petition, Praise, and Contrition.

■ Cut out the individual words, and glue one word on each side of the cube.

■ Find and cut out pictures that show what you are thankful for. Glue them on the appropriate side.

■ On a separate piece of paper, write words for things you need or names of people who need help. Cut them out and glue on the petition side.

■ On a separate piece of paper, write words that praise God. Cut the words out, and glue them on the praise side of the cube.

■ On a separate piece of paper, write two or three sentences telling God you're sorry. Cut them out, and glue them on the contrition side.

**STANDING CUBE DIRECTIONS**

1. Fold two pieces of paper leaving a ½ inch of extra space at the top.

2. Fold tabs over as if you were sealing an envelope.

3. Lightly apply glue to each tab.

4. Use the glued tabs to attach each paper to one another. Each tab should attach to the non-tabbed side of the other paper.

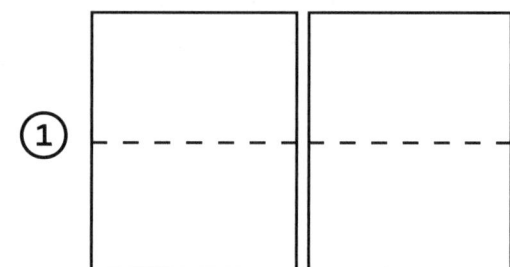

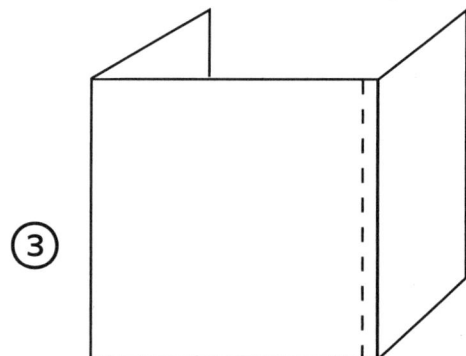

# Haiku on Watercolor Background

**CENTER TWO**

Students will learn and remember characteristics of Saint Catherine by creating this watercolor.

### DIRECTIONS

- Select a variety of watercolors and paint the paper in horizontal stripes. Be sure the colors overlap.

- While this is drying, choose one of the haikus about Catherine.

- Practice printing it on a piece of scrap paper.

- Print it neatly on the watercolor.

### HAIKUS:

*Catherine loved God*
*She was very courageous*
*Lived in Siena*

*Catherine prayed lots*
*She wanted no more fighting*
*A big peacemaker*

*Saint Catherine of Siena*

# CATECHIST PAGE FOR GRADES 4-6

## OBJECTIVES

■ *To help children learn about Saint Catherine of Siena through reading "Saint Catherine's Story"*

■ *At center one, learn the four types of prayer through making a standing cube*

■ *At center two, to review facts about Saint Catherine through writing a haiku*

## MATERIALS

■ *Variety of 11" x 17" colored paper for making standing cubes, 2 sheets for each student*

■ *Variety of magazines for cutting out pictures*

■ *Scissors*

■ *Glue*

■ *Markers for writing on standing cube and on watercolor project*

■ *Watercolors/brushes, enough for your class*

■ *Watercolor paper, one sheet per student*

## Saint Catherine's Story

**TEACHER:** Can you imagine being the youngest of 25 children? Think how many older brothers and sisters you would have to "boss" you around! Catherine was the youngest of 25 children. She was born in a northern Italian city called Siena. When she was little, she saw Jesus, who smiled at her and blessed her. When she grew up, her parents wanted her to get married, but she wanted to be a religious sister. Her parents tried to change her mind by making her do a lot of hard jobs and telling her "No" very often. Catherine would not change her mind. So, her parents gave up and Catherine became a sister.

**READER ONE:** Catherine joined the Third Order Dominican Sisters; she wore the black and white habit. Catherine spent a lot of time by herself in silence. She prayed for everyone.

One night when Catherine was praying, Jesus and the Blessed Mother appeared to her. Jesus gave her a ring. This was a symbol that Catherine was the bride of Jesus. Jesus also told her to spend more time helping people and less time praying. Catherine gave food to the poor and took the sick to the hospital. Many people saw her kindness and joined her in helping others.

**READER TWO:** During Catherine's life, the Catholic Church had many problems and there were many wars. Catherine wrote letters to the kings and queens to beg for peace. She also wrote the pope, who ran away to Avignon, France, to avoid problems. Catherine told him to return to Rome to rule the Church because this was what God wanted. Catherine was a very courageous woman who greatly influenced the politics of her time. Women did not usually impact the world like Catherine did.

**READER THREE:** Catherine died in Rome at the age of 33. She worked hard to bring peace to a world filled with fighting. Now, it was time for her to rest in the arms of God and enjoy peace forever.

# Prayer Cubes

**CENTER ONE**

Saint Catherine used the four types of prayer every day. Students will learn and remember these types of prayer through making a prayer cube, finding pictures and writing their own prayers.

**DIRECTIONS**

- Make a cube.

- On plain paper, print the words: Thanksgiving, Petition, Praise, and Contrition.

- Cut out the individual words, and glue one word on each side of the cube.

- Find and cut out pictures that show what you are thankful for. Glue them on the appropriate side.

- On a separate piece of paper, write words for things you need or names of people who need help. Cut them out and glue on the petition side.

- On a separate piece of paper, write words that praise God. Cut the words out, and glue them on the praise side of the cube.

- On a separate piece of paper, write two or three sentences telling God you're sorry. Cut them out, and glue them on the contrition side.

**STANDING CUBE DIRECTIONS**

Example:

1. Fold two pieces of paper leaving a ½ inch of extra space at the top.

2. Fold tabs over as if you were sealing an envelope.

3. Lightly apply glue to each tab.

4. Use the glued tabs to attach each paper to one another. Each tab should attach to the non-tabbed side of the other paper.

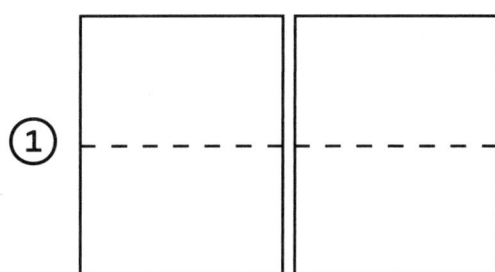

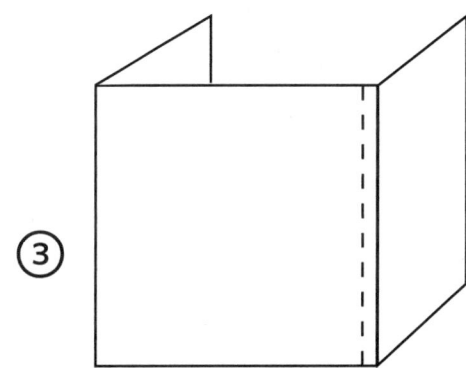

*Saint Catherine of Siena* 57

# Haiku on Watercolor Background

**CENTER TWO**

Students will choose characteristics of Saint Catherine. Students are reminded to imitate these characteristics through writing a haiku on paper with watercolor background.

**DIRECTIONS**

■ Select a variety of colors and watercolor the paper in stripes; be sure the colors overlap.

■ While this is drying, write a haiku about Saint Catherine. After writing the haiku on a scrap sheet of paper, have an adult check it.

■ Print it neatly on the watercolor. Here is the form and a sample for a haiku:

1st line: 5 syllables — *Catherine loved God*
2nd line: 7 syllables — *She was very courageous*
3rd line: 5 syllables — *Lived in Siena*

58 Learning Centers: Saints

# Saint Damien Joseph de Veuster

*Feastday: May 10*

## CATECHIST PAGE FOR GRADES 1-3

### OBJECTIVES

- *To help children understand the life of Father Damien through reading "Saint Damien's Story"*
- *At center one, create a stained glass window with symbols that represent Father Damien's life*
- *At center two, design a church using common items found in a church*

### MATERIALS

- *Tissue paper (variety of colors) for stained-glass windows*
- *Glue mixed with water*
- *Stained-glass window template, two for each student, found on page 61*
- *Markers for making sections in stained- glass windows*

Each student needs one of each of the following items:

- *Scissors*
- *Cereal box*

## Saint Damien's Story

I, Jozef De Veuster was born in the village of Tremelo in Belgium on January 3, 1840. I had six brothers and sisters. We liked to play together. When I grew up I became a religious brother and was given the name Brother Damien. I prayed every day that I could be a missionary and one day my prayer was answered and I was sent to Hawaii. I studied and became a priest; then everyone called me Father Damien.

At this time, there was a terrible disease called leprosy. If someone had this disease, he/she could no longer live with his/her family. This person had to live on a special island with other people who had this disease. I told the bishop I would live on this special island even though I did not have the disease so I could help people.

I knew I might catch the disease and die but I wanted all of these people to know how much God loved them. I was scared, but I was brave. I helped the people by building a hospital. After a while, I caught the disease. I continued to help people until I was very sick. Sister Marianne Cope took care of me while I was sick and continued my work after I died.

*Saint Damien Joseph de Veuster* 59

## CENTER ONE: Window of Life

Our Catholic churches often have stained glass windows, which represent important facts about a particular saint. Creating a stained glass window will enable students to choose symbols that will help them remember important facts about Father Damien.

**DIRECTIONS**

- Cut off the front panel from the cereal box. Glue a copy of the window template, found on page 62, on the front panel.

- Cut out the shape.

- Tear the tissue paper into small pieces, but large enough to write something or draw a picture on it. Glue the tissue paper on the template. Be sure to overlap the pieces. Let it dry.

- Use a black permanent marker, and go over the lines so you can see the sections of the stained glass window.

- In each section write a word or draw a picture that reminds you of Father Damien.

## CENTER TWO: Design a Church

Not only did Father Damien build a hospital, he also built a church. Students will learn the names of important artifacts found in churches as they design their own church.

**DIRECTIONS**

- Cut off the front of the cereal box. (Used for the window of Life)

- Add designs on the walls of your church.

- Cut out the church templates. Color and glue them in the correct places.

- Enjoy your church!

ITEMS FOUND IN A CHURCH

*Saint Damien Joseph de Veuster*

## CATECHIST'S PAGE GRADES 4-6

**OBJECTIVES**

- *To help children understand the life of Father Damien through reading "Saint Damien's Story"*

- *At center one, to create stained-glass windows with symbols that represent Father Damien's life and the student's life*

- *At center two, to design a church using common items found in a church*

**MATERIALS**

- *Tissue paper (variety of colors) for stained-glass windows*

- *Glue mixed with water*

- *Stained-glass window template, two for each student, found on page 62*

- *Markers for making sections in stained-glass windows*

Each student needs one of each of the following items:

- *Scissors*

- *Cereal box*

# Father Damien's Story

**READER ONE:** Jozef De Veuster was born on January 3, 1840 in the village of Tremelo in Belgium. Six brothers and sisters welcomed him into the world. Jozef and his brothers and sisters enjoyed playing together. In 1860, he entered the Picpus Brothers and took the name of Brother Damien. While Brother Damien was studying for the priesthood, he prayed daily to be sent on a mission. Brother Damien was sent to Honolulu as a missionary. He finished his studies and was ordained in 1864.

**READER TWO:** At this time, there was a terrible disease called leprosy. People believed back then that it was very contagious. If someone had this disease, he/she was not allowed to live with their families or work with others. He/She was taken to an island in Hawaii (Moloka'i), where only people who had this disease lived. There was no one there to help them, and it was difficult for them to help each other because of their illness.

**READER THREE:** Bishop Maigret felt sorry for the lepers. He thought they should be able to attend Mass and receive the sacraments. He also knew if he sent a priest to help them, the priest might become sick with leprosy and die. The bishop asked Father Damien if he wanted to volunteer for this scary job, and Damien said, "Yes."

**READER FOUR:** Father Damien and the lepers built houses and a church. He taught them how to garden. The people loved Father Damien because they knew he would help them in anyway he could. Father Damien felt ill and went to the doctor. He was diagnosed with leprosy. Now, he was like everyone else on the island.

**READER FIVE:** Eventually, he became so sick he had to stay in bed. Father Damien grew weaker and weaker. He died in 1889 at the age of 49. Many people felt sad. To this day, Father Damien's love and compassion are remembered on the island of Moloka'i.

*Saint Damien Joseph de Veuster*

## CENTER ONE: Windows of Life

Our Catholic churches often have stained-glass windows, which represent important facts about a particular saint. Creating a stained-glass window will enable students to choose symbols that will help them remember important facts about Father Damien.

**DIRECTIONS**

- Cut off the front panel from the cereal box. Glue the window template on the front panel.
- Cut out the shape.
- Tear the tissue paper into small pieces but large enough to write something on it or draw a picture on it. Glue it on the template. Be sure to overlap the pieces. Let it dry.
- Use a black permanent marker and go over the lines so you can see the sections of the stained-glass window.
- In each section, write a word or draw a picture that reminds you of Father Damien.
- Make a second window on the back. Glue on another window template.
- In each section, write a word or draw a picture about yourself.
- Share your windows with a friend.

## CENTER TWO: Design a Church

Not only did Father Damien help the lepers, he also helped build a hospital and a church. Students will learn the names of important artifacts found in churches as they design their own church.

**DIRECTIONS**

- Cut off the front of the cereal box. (used to make the Windows of Life)
- Add designs to the walls of the church,
- Cut out the church templates. Color and glue them in the correct places.
- Enjoy your church!

64 Learning Centers: Saints

# 10

# Saint Benedict

*Feastday: July 11*

### CATECHIST'S PAGE FOR GRADES 1-3

**OBJECTIVES**

■ *To help children understand the life of Saint Benedict through reading "Saint Benedict's Story"*

■ *At center one, to learn the word "welcome" in different languages by making a hospitality mat*

■ *At center two, to think of ways to keep Christ in the center of your life by making a Christ in the Center target.*

**MATERIALS**

■ *Word card template*

■ *Large paper for mats*

■ *Circle and arrow templates for Christ in the center target found on page 66*

■ *Brad to attach the arrow, one for each student*

■ *Markers/crayons for decorating*

■ *Glue*

## Saint Benedict's Story

I was born in central Italy in a town called Nursia (present-day Norcia). My parents were very surprised when they had twins. They named me Benedict and my sister, Scholastica. We liked to play together, but sometimes we fought.

When I was older, I studied in Rome. I was a very good student. I left Rome and lived in a cave in a small town for three years. A kind monk named Romanus brought me food and clothing. A group of men asked me to be their leader, and I wanted them to live simply and to pray often. The men did not like this so they decided to kill me. The men put poison in my wine.

When I blessed the wine, the glass broke, and I knew what the men had tried to do. I felt very sad, and I left.

I went back to live in the cave, but people saw how good and holy I was, and other men joined me. I founded an order, the Benedictines. I wrote rules that helped the men keep Christ in the center of their lives, and I also taught them how to run the monastery. Working and praying were very important to me.

I died when I was 63 years old, and I was buried with my sister, Scholastica.

*Saint Benedict*

# Hospitality Mats

Saint Benedict was known for his hospitality. The hospitality mats will help students be aware of different ways they can be hospitable to everyone, just like Saint Benedict.

**DIRECTIONS**

- Get a large sheet of paper.
- Cut out the word cards that mean welcome.
- Color the words.
- On another piece of paper, write a sentence about how you can welcome someone. Cut it out and glue the sentence to the mat.
- Glue the word cards around the sentence.
- Decorate the mat.

VELKOMMEN

BIENVENIDOS

WELCOME

SHALOM

BIENVENUE

ALOHA

# Christ in the Center Target

Saint Benedict made Jesus the center of his life. This target will help students practice making Jesus the center of their lives each day.

**DIRECTIONS**

■ Cut out the circle and arrow template on page 70.

■ In each section on the circle, draw pictures or write words of how you will keep Christ in the center of your life. You might draw yourself praying or sharing something or being a good friend to someone else.

■ Attach the arrow to the target with a brad. Each day put the arrow on the picture that you are going to do that day to grow closer to Christ.

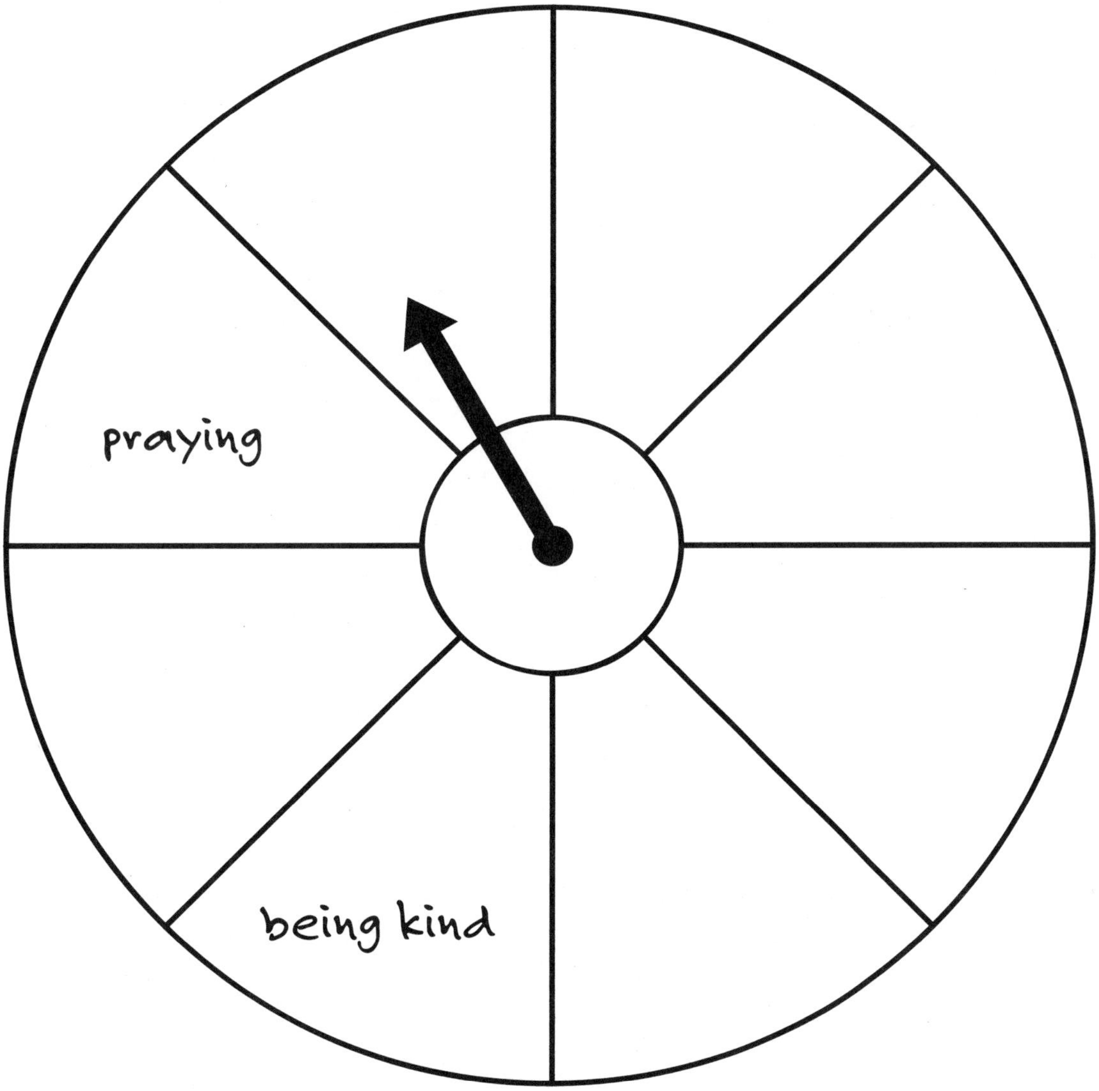

*Saint Benedict* 67

# CATECHIST'S PAGE FOR GRADES 4-6

**OBJECTIVES**

- *To help children understand the life of Saint Benedict through reading "Saint Benedict's Story"*

- *At center one, to create a dialogue poem between work and prayer*

- *At center two, to think of ways to keep Christ in the center of your life*

**MATERIALS**

- *Circle and arrow templates found on page 70 for Christ in the center target and arrow template*

- *Markers/crayons for decorating*

- *Glue*

- *Paper for poem*

## Saint Benedict's Story

**READER ONE:** A long time ago, twins were born to a Roman noble family; these children were Benedict and Scholastica. Benedict studied in Rome and was a good student.

**READER TWO:** Benedict left Rome and lived in a cave in Subiaco for three years. While he was there, a monk, Romanus, brought him food and clothing. A small group of monks discovered Benedict and asked him to be their spiritual leader. Benedict said, "Yes." But after living with him for a while, these monks decided he was asking them to pray too much and to keep too much silence.

**READER THREE:** They got together and decided to put poison in his wine to kill him. One of the monks put poison in his wine, and when Benedict blessed the wine, the glass broke. He immediately knew what the monks had tried to do. He told the monks that he was leaving and that they should find someone else to be their leader. He returned to the cave.

**READER FOUR:** Benedict was not to live the life of a hermit. Other people saw his goodness and his holiness. Other good men wanted to join him, and he became their leader. He also wrote a rule (The Rule of Saint Benedict), which was divided into two sections. The first section told the men how to keep Christ in the center of their lives, and the second section told the men how to run the monastery.

**READER FIVE:** Benedict and his monks served others. They helped people learn how to do different types of work. They also taught people about God and how to pray. Once while Benedict was praying, he "knew" that another man fell into the lake and was drowning. He sent a monk to rescue the man. The monk was so excited he ran across the water and grabbed the man by his hair to pull him out of the lake. Only when both men returned to shore, did the monk who "walked on water" realize what he did. Benedict died at the age of 63.

# Dialogue Poem

Saint Benedict believed that work and prayer were very important. Creating a dialogue poem will help students see the importance of both of these values.

**DIRECTIONS**

- Think about work.
- Create a graphic organizer with words about work.
- Think about prayer.
- Create a graphic organizer with words about prayer.
- Using your words, create a dialogue poem.
- There will be two lines in every stanza.
- The first line will be about work; the second line will be about prayer.

**SAMPLE POEM:**

I am work
*I am prayer*

I am five days a week
*I am whenever you want*

I am a source of money
*I am a source of hope*

I help others
*I do too!*

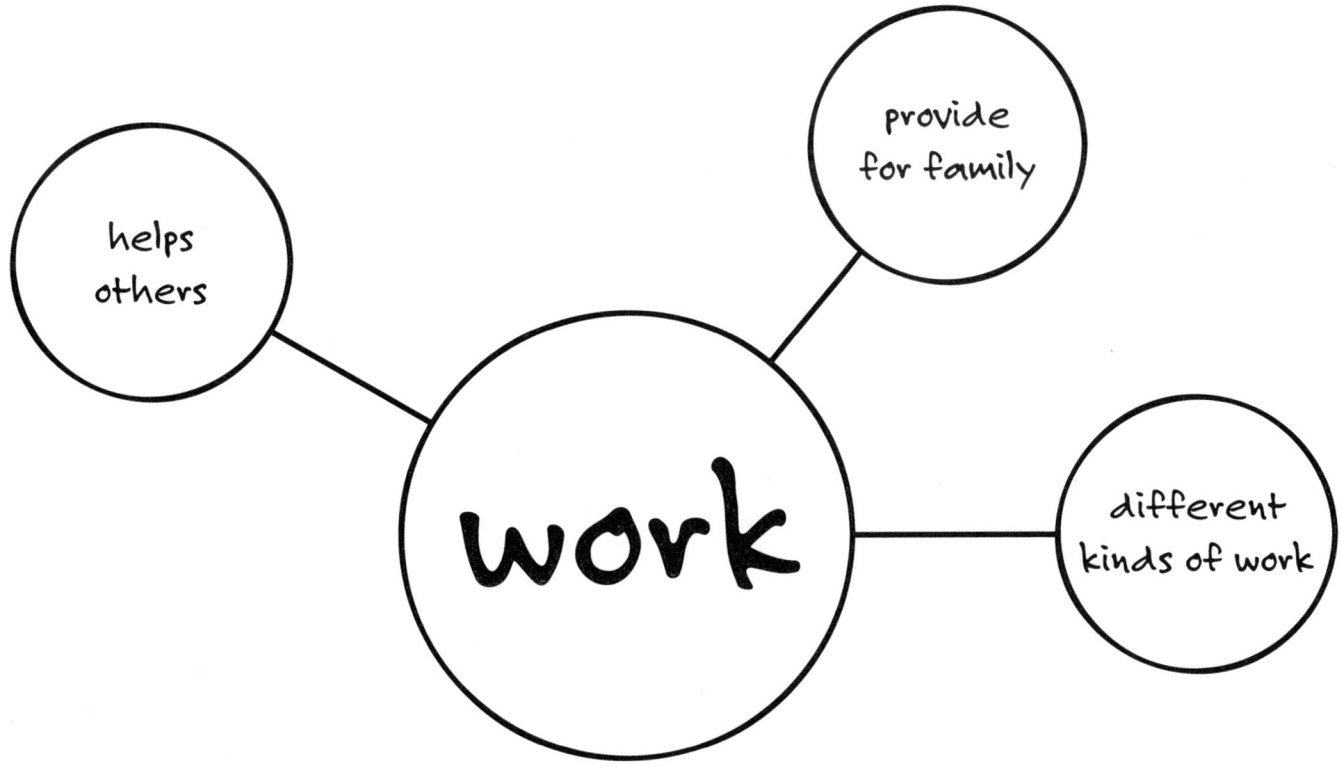

Saint Benedict 69

# Christ in the Center Target

**CENTER TWO**

Saint Benedict made Jesus the center of his life. This target will help students practice making Jesus the center of their lives each day.

**DIRECTIONS**

- Cut out the target template.

- Draw pictures in each section of how you will keep Christ in the center of your life. You might draw a person praying, or someone sharing, or someone being a good friend to someone else.

- Cut out the paper arrow. Attach it to the target with a brad. Each day put the arrow on the picture that you are going to do that day to grow closer to Christ.

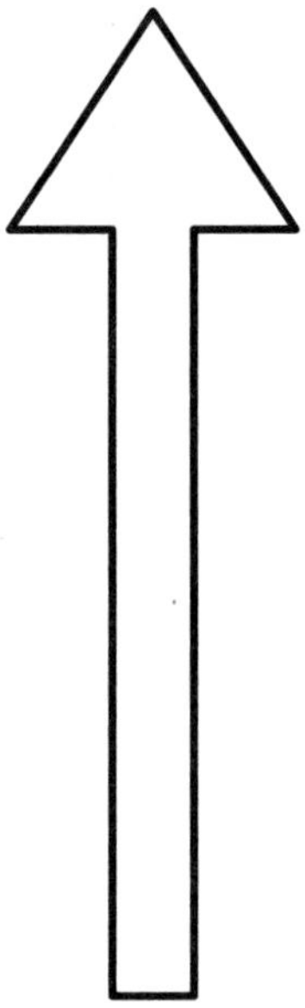

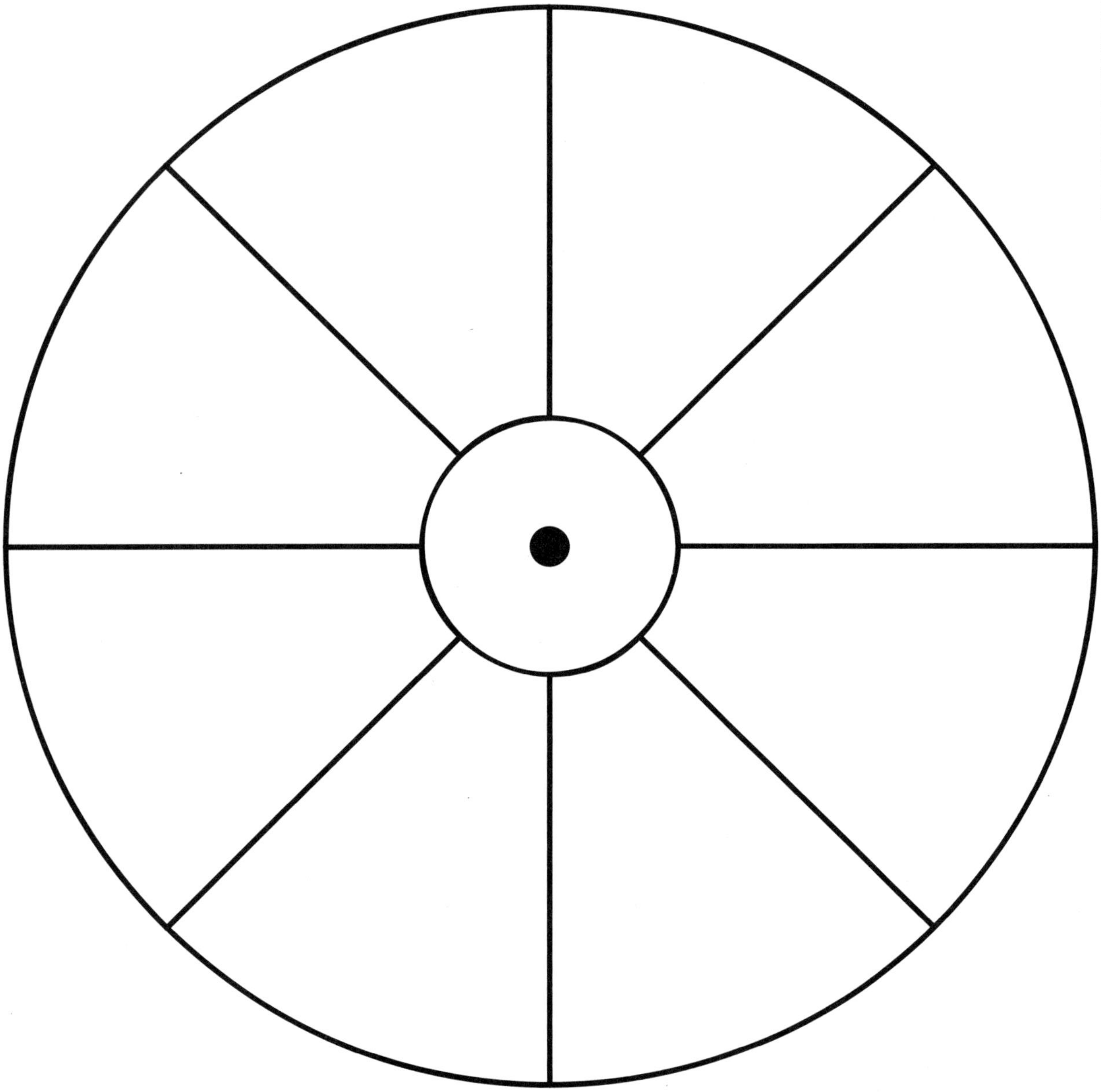

70 Learning Centers: Saints

# Saint Kateri Tekakwitha

*Feastday: July 14*

### CATECHIST PAGE FOR GRADES 1-3

### OBJECTIVES

- *To help children learn about Saint Kateri Tekakwitha through reading "Saint Kateri's Story"*
- *At center one, help children create a baptismal totem pole as a reminder of baptismal symbols*
- *At center two, help children sequence events of Kateri's life using a card sort*

### MATERIALS

Each student needs one of each of the following items:

- *Empty paper towel rolls for baptismal totem pole*
- *Copy of Baptismal Symbols template, found on page 72*
- *Set of 10 cards per student for Card sort*
- *Tempera paint, variety of colors*
- *Glue*
- *Crayons and markers for decorating*

## Saint Kateri's Story

I was born near Auriesville, New York. I was named "Tekakwitha," which means, "She puts things in order." I grew up in a very orderly home. As the white people came across the ocean from Europe, they brought illnesses with them. My parents caught a disease and died.

My uncle adopted me. I also caught a disease, but I did not die. The disease left marks on my face and hurt my eyes; I could not see very well, but I helped by planting corn and gathering firewood.

One day, missionaries arrived wearing "black robes." We nicknamed them "Black Robes." These men taught us about Jesus. I listened carefully. I decided to be baptized a Catholic.

My uncle did not want me to do this, but I was baptized and was given the name "Kateri." The other Native Americans made fun of me and teased me. I decided to leave the village.

I went to live at a Jesuit mission where I continued to learn more about God. I continued to work hard and pray. People often felt closer to God when they were with me when I prayed.

I became very sick. I knew I was dying. After I died, the people noticed my face no longer had marks on it but that it was silky and smooth. This sign told everyone of my great love for God.

*Saint Kateri Tekakwitha*

# Baptismal Totem Poles

Saint Kateri was baptized when she was older. Students will learn about the baptismal symbols through making the totem pole.

**DIRECTIONS**

- Paint the paper towel roll.
- Color and cut out the baptismal symbols.
- Glue the symbols on the totem pole.

72 Learning Centers: Saints

# Card Sort

**CENTER TWO**

"Tekakwitha" means "she puts things in order;" so all students can imitate Kateri in this activity.

**DIRECTIONS**

■ Each student will be given a set of 10 cards. Each card has a phrase on it about Kateri.

■ The students must order the cards in correct sequence.

| | | |
|---|---|---|
| | Kateri catches a disease. | Kateri's parents die from disease. |
| | Kateri's village made fun of her for being baptized. | Kateri was baptized by Jesuit priests. |
| Kateri grew up in the Mohawk village. | Kateri died April 17, 1680. | Kateri was born in 1656. |
| Jesuit priests visit Kateri's village. | Kateri leaves her tribe. | Kateri's scars are healed after death. |

*Saint Kateri Tekakwitha*

# CATECHIST PAGE FOR GRADES 4-6

## OBJECTIVES

- To help children learn about Saint Kateri Tekakwitha through reading "Saint Kateri's Story"

- At center one, help children create a baptismal totem pole as a reminder of baptismal symbols

- At center two, children will remember events of Kateri's life by making a Wordle

## MATERIALS

Each student needs one of each of the following items:

- Empty paper towel rolls for baptismal totem pole

- A copy of the baptismal symbols template on page 72.

- Tempera paint—a variety of colors

- Glue

- Scissors

- Access to a computer for Wordle

- Variety of colored construction paper for completed Wordle

## Saint Kateri's Story

**READER ONE:** A long, long time ago, the United States had mostly Native Americans living in it and very few white people. One day in a Mohawk village, a beautiful baby girl papoose was born, who was named "Tekakwitha," which means, "She puts things in order."

**READER TWO:** As the white people came across the ocean from Europe, they brought diseases with them. Tekakwitha's parents caught the sickness and died. Tekakwitha also caught the sickness but she did not die. Her face was scared and she couldn't see well. Her uncle adopted her. Tekakwitha planted corn in the fields, gathered firewood, and carried water. She believed it was important to work hard.

**READER THREE:** One day some Jesuit priests, who were wearing black robes, arrived to visit the village. The Native Americans nicknamed the missionaries "Black Robes." They taught the people about Jesus. Tekakwitha listened carefully and decided she wanted to be baptized a Catholic. Her uncle did not want her to do this. Tekakwitha was baptized and named "Kateri."

**READER FOUR:** The other Native Americans made fun of her and teased her. The Native Americans thought she gave up her Native American ways and followed the ways of the white men. It was not easy for Kateri to stay with her tribe.

**READER FIVE:** Kateri decided to leave the village. She went to live at a Jesuit mission, where she continued to learn more about God. People often felt closer to God when they were with her when she prayed. Kateri always looked for ways to help others.

# Baptismal Totem Poles

Saint Kateri was baptized when she was older. Students will learn about the baptismal symbols through making the totem pole.

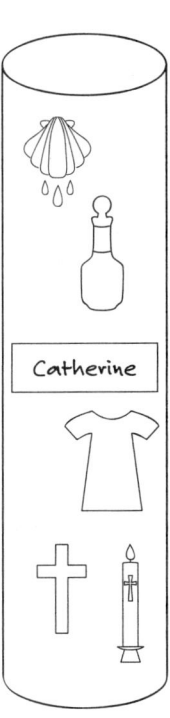

### DIRECTIONS

- Paint the paper towel roll.
- Glue a decorated 2 x 5 piece of paper with your baptismal name to the pole.
- Look up your baptismal name. Print the meaning of it under your name.
- Use marker and/or crayons to decorate all of the baptismal symbols and then cut them out.
- Glue these to the totem pole.

# Wordle Frames

Students will remember important facts about Saint Kateri through making a Wordle frame.

### DIRECTIONS

- On the computer, go to www.Wordle.net
- Choose 10-15 words from the story.
- Put them in Wordle.
- Print out your Wordle.
- Get a large piece of construction paper
- Center and glue your Wordle on it.

*Saint Kateri Tekakwitha*

# Saint Dominic

*Feastday: August 8*

### CATECHIST'S PAGE GRADES 1-3

**OBJECTIVES**

■ Help children understand Saint Dominic's life through reading "Saint Dominic's Story"

■ At center one, to help children know what they believe about God through making a belief shield

■ At center two, to help children learn the sequential order of Psalm 23

**MATERIALS**

■ Belief shield template found on page 77

■ Construction paper for shield

■ Markers, pens, and pencils

■ Sets of sheep templates found on page 78 for Psalm unscramble

■ Glue

## Saint Dominic's Story

Did you ever wonder if some mothers dreamed about their children before they were born? My mother, Jane, dreamed about me before I was born. In her dream, my mother saw a dog running with a burning torch setting the world aflame. When I was born and I had two older brothers and a sister. I lived with my family until I was seven years old.

When I turned seven, my father sent me to live with my uncle who was a priest. My uncle taught me how to read using the Psalms. I studied to become a priest. I lived a very simple life. I slept on the floor rather than in a bed. I ate very little and give most of my food to the poor.

I was known as an outstanding preacher. People came to hear me and many people believed the truth that I taught. In 1206, on a hill in France, I saw a globe of fire descend upon a shrine of Our Lady. I understood that I was to start a monastery of nuns at Prouille.

I also established a monastery for men next to the women. My mother's dream came true. I went many places bringing the light of truth. Throughout my whole life, I wanted people to know who God really was. As I became older, I began to slow down and became ill. I died on August 6, 1221.

76 Learning Centers: Saints

# Belief Shields

Saint Dominic helped people understand the truth about God. Our Catholic faith teaches us many things about God. The shield will help students remember some of these important facts.

**DIRECTIONS**

■ Cut out the Dominican shield. Glue it on construction paper.

■ Write three things in the center of the shield that you know to be true about God.

Here are some examples: *There are three persons in one God.*

*God sent us Jesus to show us God's love.*

*God always was, and always will be.*

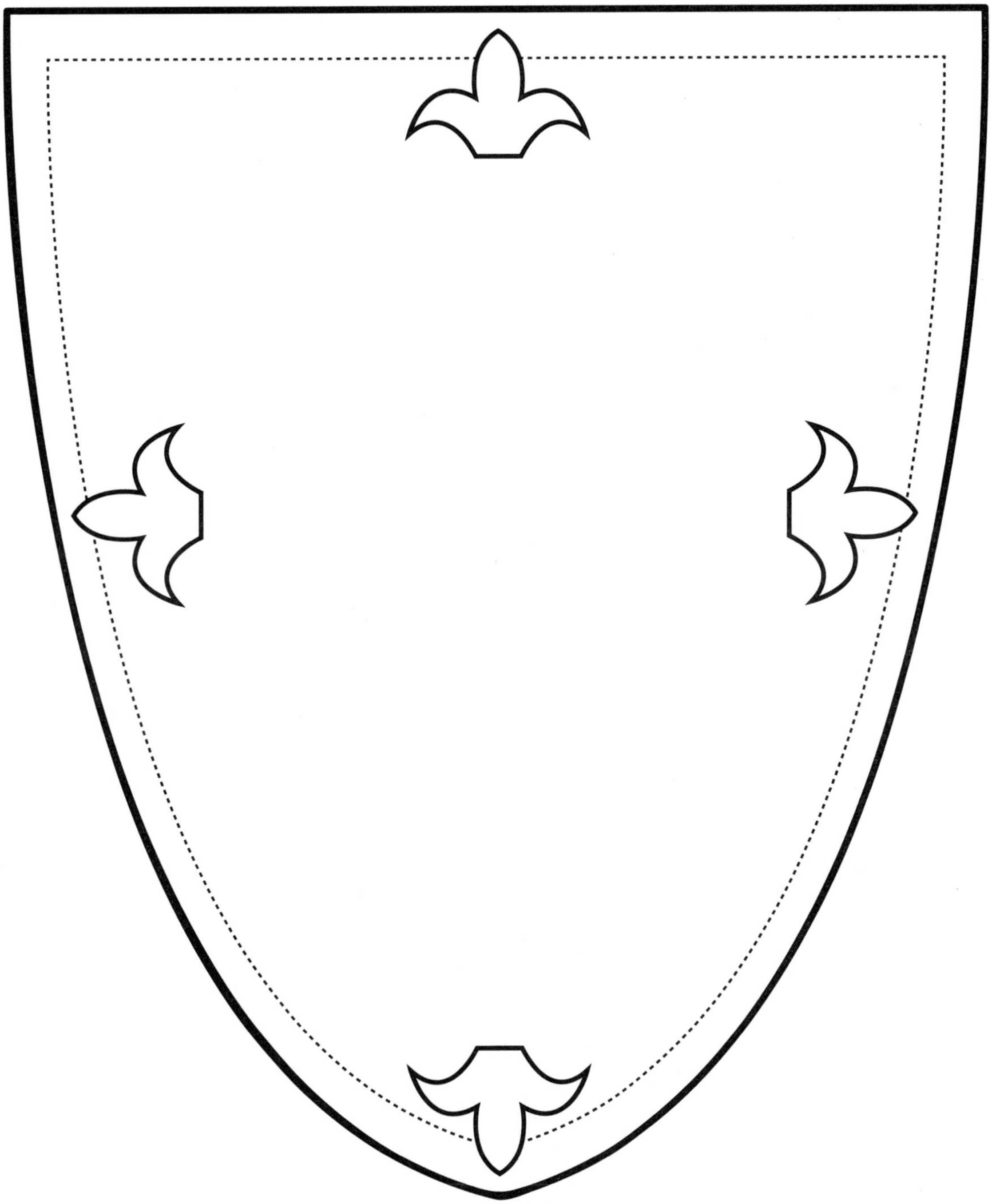

Saint Dominic 77

# Psalm Unscramble

**CENTER TWO**

Saint Dominic learned to read using the Psalms. Psalm 23 will help students practice their reading skills as they put the sheep in sequential order.

**DIRECTIONS**

- Color the sheep and cut out the squares of sheep.
- Put the sheep in correct order and pray Psalm 23.

| | | |
|---|---|---|
| The Lord is my Shepherd, I shall not want | For you are with me; | He makes me lie down in green pastures |
| He leads me beside still waters | And I shall dwell in the House of the Lord | He restores my soul |
| You prepare a table before me in the presence of my enemies | Surely goodness and mercy shall follow me All the days of my life. My whole life long. | You anoint my head with oil; my cup overflows |
| Even though I walk through the darkest valley, I fear no evil | He restores my soul. He leads me in the right paths for His Name's sake | Your rod and Your staff - they comfort me. |

78 Learning Centers: Saints

# CATECHIST'S PAGE GRADES 4-6

**OBJECTIVES**

■ *Help children understand Saint Dominic's life through reading "Saint Dominic's Story"*

■ *At center one, to help children know what they believe about God through making a belief shield*

■ *At center two, to help children learn about the Book of Psalms and then write their own psalm.*

**MATERIALS**

■ *Belief shield template found on page 77.*

■ *Construction paper for shield*

■ *Markers, pens, and pencils for writing*

■ *Scroll template, found on page 81, two per student*

## Saint Dominic's Story

**READER ONE:** Did you ever wonder if some mothers dream about their children before they are born? Dominic's mother, Jane, had a dream about him before he was born. In her dream, Jane saw a dog running with a burning torch setting the world aflame. Dominic was born in 1170 in Spain; Dominic had two older brothers, Anthony and Mannes as well as a sister. Dominic lived with his family until he was seven years old; then he lived with his uncle, who was a priest. His uncle taught him how to read using the Psalms.

**READER TWO:** Dominic studied to become a priest. While at Palencia, he lived a very simple life. He slept on the floor rather than in a bed and, he ate very little, giving most of his food to the poor.

**READER THREE:** In 1203, Father Dominic went with one of his friends, Bishop Don Diego, to a wedding. As they were going through Toulouse, they heard a lie—some people were saying that all material things were bad. The innkeeper where Bishop Don Diego and Dominic were staying believed this. Dominic presented outstanding facts and arguments, and soon converted the innkeeper to the Catholic faith. At that time, the pope asked the Cistercian abbots to preach against the lies. Bishop Don Diego and Dominic joined them, and Father Dominic became known as Brother Dominic.

**READER FOUR:** Brother Dominic was known as an outstanding preacher. People came to hear him, and many people believed the truth that he taught. As he worked with the group of men preaching against the lie, he wondered if God was calling him to go to a different place.

**READER FIVE:** In 1206, on a hill of Fanjeaux, overlooking Prouille, Dominic saw a globe of fire descend upon a shrine of Our Lady. He saw this sign not one night, but three nights! He understood that he was to start a monastery of nuns at Prouille.

*Saint Dominic*

Dominic also established a monastery for men next to the women. The Dominicans are unusual for a couple of reasons: 1) The contemplative women's monastery was founded first. Dominic knew that in order to be successful as a preacher, others needed to pray for the preacher. 2) The main work of the Dominicans is to preach. Preaching is done by both word and example.

**READER SIX:** Dominic's mother's dream came true. Her son went many places bringing the light of truth to those who believed the lie. Throughout his whole life, Dominic wanted people to know who God really was. As he became older, he began to slow down and became ill. Dominic died on August 6, 1221.

# Belief Shields

Saint Dominic helped people understand the truth about God. Our Catholic faith teaches us many things about God. The shield will help students remember some of these important facts.

## DIRECTIONS

Follow the directions on page 77, except write five beliefs on the shield.

# Psalms of Yesterday and Today

Saint Dominic learned to read using the Psalms. Students will practice their reading and writing skills through writing their own psalm.

## DIRECTIONS

- Cut out two scroll templates.
- Write your favorite psalm from the Bible on one scroll.
- Write you own psalm on one scroll.
- Decorate the scrolls.
- Share your psalm with your classmates.

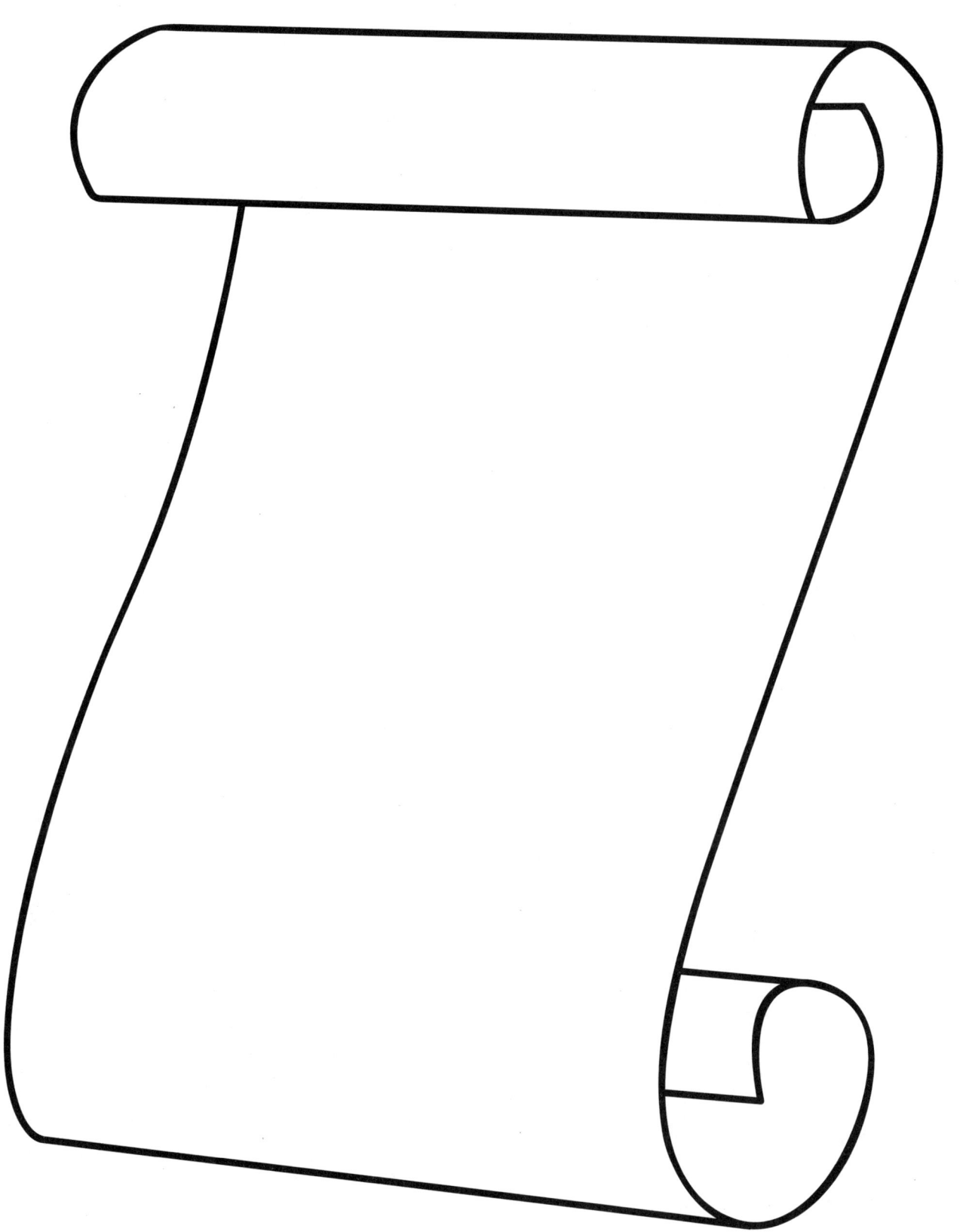

# Saint Edith Stein

*Feastday: August 9*

## CATECHIST'S PAGE GRADES 1-3

### OBJECTIVES

- *To help children understand the life of Edith Stein through reading "Saint Edith's Story"*
- *At center one, to help children to understand the menorah by making one*
- *At center two, to help children understand four Hanukkah facts by making a Star of David mobile*

### MATERIALS

- *Star of David template found on page 84.*
- *Yarn for mobile*
- *Pens, markers, scissors, glue*
- *Hanukkah fact sheet*

FOR MENORAH

- *1, ten-inch poster board circle*
- *Aluminum foil*
- *9 small craft sticks*
- *1 large craft stick*
- *Facial tissue for Menorah*
- *Yellow tissue paper for Menorah*
- *White tempera paint*

## Saint Edith's Story

I was born in Breslav, Germany on October 12, 1891. I was the youngest of 11 children. My parents, who were devout Jews, named me Edith. My father died when I was little so my mother had to work. My sister took care of all of us. I was friendly and I loved to laugh. My classmates enjoyed hanging out with me. I loved to read both at home and at school, which made me very smart.

For a little while, I stopped believing in God, but I didn't want my family to know so I still attended Sabbath services each week.

One day, I began reading the New Testament, a part of the Catholic Bible. As I read, I started believing in God. I was baptized a Catholic.

I became a religious sister and my new name was Sister Teresia Benedicta of the Cross.

In 1933, Adolf Hitler and his soldiers began to attack the Jewish people. They believed the Jewish people were bad. Hitler and his soldiers captured and killed me because I was a Jew. I died on August 7, 1942.

82 Learning Centers: Saints

# Star of David Mobile

**CENTER ONE**

Our Catholic faith is rooted in Judaism. Saint Edith was Jewish before she became a Catholic. Students will learn about Hanukkah, one of the Jewish festivals, by making the Star of David mobile.

**DIRECTIONS**

- Cut out the large Star of David template.
- Punch four holes; one on each outside triangle tip.
- Decorate the Star of David template.
- Cut out each fact from the fact sheet.
- Hang from the Star of David.

> **Hanukkah is sometimes calls the Festival of Lights and is celebrated by the Jewish people.**

> **Hanukkah is celebrated for eight days.**

> **A menorah is used to celebrate Hanukkah. One candle is lit each night.**

> **Small gifts are given each night to each person in the family.**

*Saint Edith Stein*

# Menorah

**CENTER TWO**

Students will realize the Jewish faith has important symbols just like the Catholic faith. Students will create a menorah and learn that it is an important symbol in the Jewish faith.

**DIRECTIONS**

- Cut the circle in half. Cover each half with aluminum foil.

- Cover the large craft stick in aluminum foil.

- Paint the small crafts sticks white.

- Cut the tissue paper into 1-inch squares. Roll it to make a flame.

- Glue flames at the end of the white craft sticks.

- After these have dried, glue one of the white sticks at the straight side, in the center. Most of the stick should stick out; only glue a small section to the circle.

- Glue four more sticks to the left of this center stick. These sticks should be a little lower than the center stick.

- Glue four more sticks to the right of the center stick. These sticks should be the same height as the four sticks to the left.

- Glue the big stick at the center of the rounded side of the circle.

- Glue the bottom of the rounded ends together. Stuff with facial tissue. Glue the circles closed on all sides.

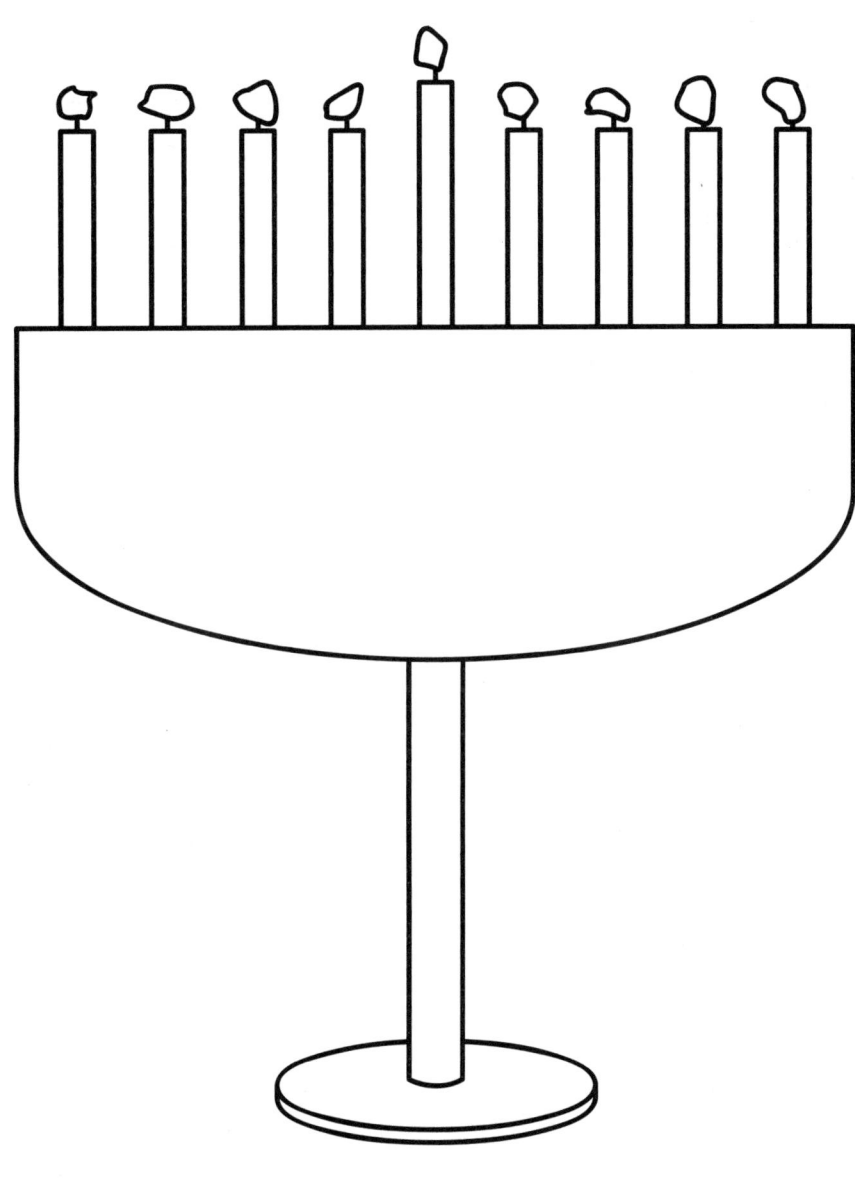

*Saint Edith Stein*

# CATECHIST'S PAGE GRADES 4-6

**OBJECTIVES**

■ *To help children understand the life of Edith Stein through reading "Saint Edith's Story"*

■ *At center one, to help children understand the menorah by making one*

■ *At center two, to help children understand Jewish symbols (Mezuzah, Torah, Star of David, and Menorah through researching and making a mobile*

**MATERIALS**

FOR MOBILE

■ *Star of David template, found on page 84 and Jewish symbols template found on page 87.*

■ *Yarn*

■ *Pens, markers*

FOR MENORAH

■ *1 ten-inch poster board circle*

■ *Aluminum foil*

■ *9 small craft sticks*

■ *1 large craft stick*

■ *Facial tissue*

■ *Yellow tissue paper*

■ *White tempera paint*

■ *Scissors*

■ *Glue*

## Saint Edith's Story

**READER ONE:** Edith Stein was born on October 12, 1891. Her father and mother were devout Jews. Her father died when Edith was a year old. Her mother took care of the family business so her older sister babysat Edith and the other children.

**READER TWO:** When Edith turned 13, she suddenly stopped believing in God. She still attended Sabbath services because she didn't want her family to know she was struggling with her faith. In 1917, Edith began reading the New Testament, a part of the Catholic Bible. As she read, she found herself believing in God. Edith was baptized Catholic and was happy with her new faith.

**READER THREE:** In 1933, Adolf Hitler and his soldiers began to attack the Jewish people because they believed the Jewish people were bad. Edith was fired from her job because she was Jewish. Edith joined the Discalced Carmelites in 1933 and was given the name Sr. Teresia Benedicta of the Cross. As Hitler and his soldiers became more powerful, Sr. Teresia Benedicta of the Cross knew she wasn't safe living in Germany. She and her sister Rosa, moved to the Netherlands.

**READER FOUR:** In 1942, Hitler and his soldiers began capturing Jews in the Netherlands. Sr. Teresia Benedicta of the Cross and Rosa tried to go to Switzerland where they could be safe again. They could not get travel passes. Hitler and his soldiers captured both of them.

They were put on trains and taken to a camp in Poland. Sr. Teresia Benedicta of the Cross died on August 9, 1942.

**CENTER ONE**

# Jewish Symbols

Our Catholic faith is rooted in Judaism. Saint Edith was Jewish before she became a Catholic. Students will learn about several Jewish symbols by making the Star of David mobile.

**DIRECTIONS**

- Cut out each Jewish symbol.
- On the back of each symbol, write a fact about it.
- Punch a hole in the outside triangle tip on the Star of David.
- Hang each symbol using yarn.

**Star of David**

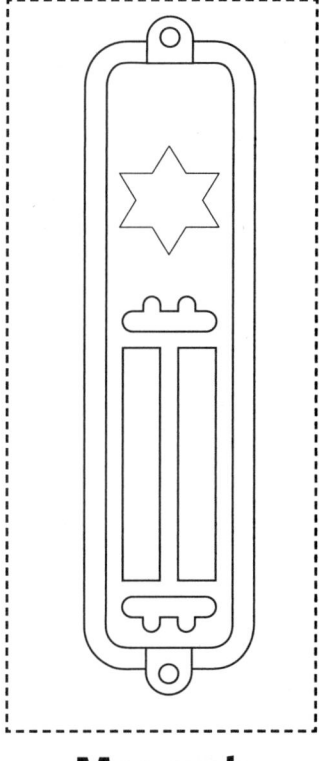

**Mezuzah**

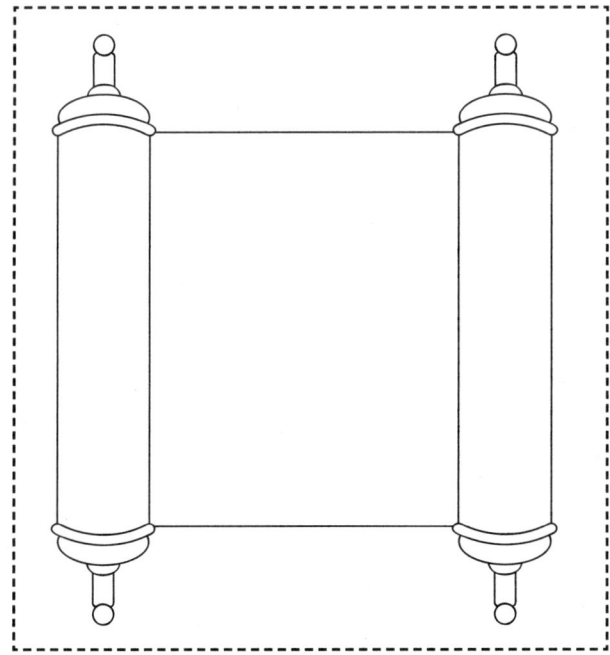

**Torah**

**Menorah**

*Saint Edith Stein* **87**

# Menorah

**CENTER TWO**

Students will realize the Jewish faith has important symbols just like the Catholic faith. Students will create a menorah and learn that it is an important symbol in the Jewish faith.

## DIRECTIONS

■ Cut the circle in half. Cover each half in aluminum foil.

■ Cover the large craft stick in aluminum foil.

■ Paint the small craft sticks white.

■ Cut the tissue paper into 1-inch squares. Roll it to make a flame.

■ Glue flames at the end of the white craft sticks.

■ After these have dried, glue one of the white sticks at the straight side, in the center. Most of the stick should stick out. Only glue a small section to the circle.

■ Glue four more sticks to the left of this center stick. These sticks should be a little lower than the center stick.

■ Glue four more sticks to the right of the center stick. These sticks should be the same height as the four sticks to the left.

■ Glue the big stick at the center of the rounded side of the circle.

■ Glue the bottom of the round ends together. Stuff with facial tissue. Glue the circles closed on all sides.

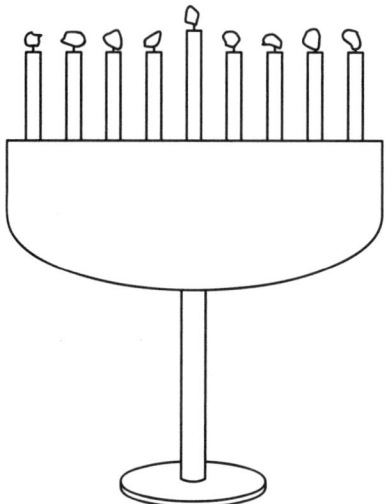

# Saint Peter Claver

*Feastday: September 9*

---

**CATECHIST PAGES FOR GRADES 1-3**

---

**OBJECTIVES**

- To learn about Saint Peter's life through "Saint Peter Claver's Story"
- At center one, to learn the eight beatitudes by making bee beatitudes
- At center two, to do acts of kindness by making chains of kindness

**MATERIALS**

For each student, have one of each of the following:

- Small flowerpot
- Flower and bees template found on page 90
- 8 Craft sticks
- Clay

ALSO NEEDED:

- Glue
- Strips of colored paper for chains of kindness

## Saint Peter's Story

I was born in Spain. I wanted to be a priest and missionary. In 1610 I left for Colombia, South America. In Colombia, I saw huge ships come in from Africa. The ships had hundreds of black slaves on them, who would be sold.

I helped these slaves and brought medicine to them. I also gave them food and clothes. I taught the slaves about God's love for them and how important they were to God. I even baptized some of them.

I did this hard work for over 40 years. Some people thought that the slaves would not go to Mass or pray as I taught them. But I continued to teach them and believed they would practice their faith.

I became very sick, and for four years I was unable to take care of the slaves who came on the boats. During that time, everyone forgot about me and the good work I did.

On September 8, 1654, I died suddenly. All at once everyone remembered me and the good work I did.

*Saint Peter Claver* 89

## CENTER ONE: Bee Beatitudes

Saint Peter Claver taught the slaves about the beatitudes. Students will remember these by making the bees.

**DIRECTIONS**

- Cut out the flower and trace seven more on colored paper.
- Cut out the flowers.
- Glue flowers on craft sticks.
- Color the bees and cut them out.
- Glue the bees on the flowers.
- Put clay in the flowerpot.
- Stick in bees and flowers.

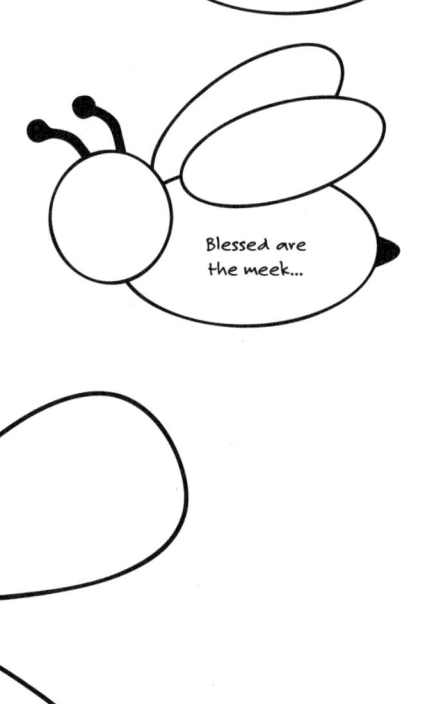

90 Learning Centers: Saints

## CENTER TWO: Chains of Kindness

The slaves came from Africa chained together on a boat. Saint Peter Claver taught the slaves about the kindness of God and others. Students will remember how the slaves were chained together and will practice acts of kindness.

**DIRECTIONS**

- Think of 10 ways you can be kind.

- Write one way on each strip.

- The first time you do one of the acts of kindness, glue the ends together to make a circle.

- The next time you do one, interlock the strip into the circle.

- Continue until your chain is finished.

*Clean up my neighborhood park*

Saint Peter Claver 91

# CATECHIST PAGES FOR GRADES 4-6

**OBJECTIVES**

■ *To learn about Saint Peter's life through "Saint Peter Claver's Story"*

■ *At center one, to learn the eight beatitudes through writing a story using Storybird*

■ *At center two, to remember facts about Saint Peter Claver through making trading cards*

**MATERIALS**

■ *Computers*

## Saint Peter's Story

**READER ONE:** Peter was born in Spain. He had three brothers and sisters. He was a very ordinary child, however he was very smart. His family often prayed the rosary together in the evenings. His mother died when he was young. He wanted to be a priest and missionary. He left for Colombia, South America. In Colombia, he saw a huge ship come in from Africa. It had hundreds of black slaves on it, who would be sold. Father Peter helped these slaves. He brought medicine to them. He also gave them food and clothes.

**READER TWO:** The people who bought the slaves did not respect them. The people who owned them did not give them many rights. Father Peter taught the slaves about God's love for them, and how important they were to God. He baptized some of them. His missionary work was very hard but Father Peter did it for over 40 years. Some people thought that the slaves would not go to Mass or pray as Father Peter taught them. But he continued to teach them, and believed they would practice their faith.

**READER THREE:** Father Peter loved good music, and he enjoyed providing a good meal for the poor. He often helped out in the hospital because he wanted everyone to know and love God.

**READER FOUR:** Father Peter became very sick, and for four years he was unable to take care of the slaves who came on the boat. In the meantime, everyone forgot about Father Peter and the good work he did. Suddenly, Father Peter died. All at once everyone remembered him, and the good work he did.

## "Storybird" Beatitudes

St. Peter Claver taught the slaves about the beatitudes. Students will focus on one of the beatitudes by writing a story using Storybird.

**DIRECTIONS**

- Choose one of the beatitudes; reflect on how that beatitude is lived today.
- Write a story in which the main character demonstrates that beatitude, and illustrate it using Storybird.
- Go to storybird.com.
- Share your stories with your classmates.

## St. Peter Claver "Trading Card"

Students will remember facts about St. Peter Claver by making trading cards.

**DIRECTIONS**

- Go to http://www.readwritethink.org/files/resources/interactives/trading_cards_2/
- Create a Trading Card for St. Peter Claver.
- After you have created your card, print it.
- Trade cards with your friends.

# 15

# Padre Pio

*Feastday: September 23*

---

### CATECHIST'S PAGE FOR GRADES 1-3

---

### OBJECTIVES

- *To acquaint children with Padre Pio through reading "Padre Pio's Story"*

- *At center one, to help children make a chalice to remind them to pray for those who are suffering*

- *At center two, to help children choose important words and write them in the form of a cross to remember that when we suffer we are like Jesus*

### MATERIALS

- *5 copies of the chalice pattern for each child, found on page 96*

- *Yellow paper to glue the chalices on*

- *Old magazines for cutting out pictures of people who are suffering*

- *Scissors*

- *Glue*

- *Pens for printing on the bottom of each chalice and writing words around the cross*

- *Cross template for each child found on page 97*

- *Brown paper to glue the cross template on*

## Padre Pio's Story

On May 25, 1887, I was born and named Francesco Forgione. My family attended Mass every day and prayed the rosary together in the evenings. My parents and grandparents told the children Bible stories every night. I loved playing church; I sang hymns and talked with Jesus, Mary, and my Guardian Angel.

When I grew up, I entered the Capuchin Order and received the name Brother Pio; later I became a priest. People called me Padre (which means Father) Pio. I did not like to see people suffer, so I built a hospital for the poor. I also prayed with people and visited the sick.

I received a very special gift from God. One day while I prayed, there suddenly appeared in the middle of the palms of my hands, on the bottoms of my feet, and in my side, red marks that caused a lot of pain. These marks were like the wounds in Jesus' hands, feet and side.

When I knew I was dying, I held a rosary in my hands. I said, "I see two mothers" (my own mother and Mary). A smile crossed my face, and then I died.

---

94 Learning Centers: Saints

### CENTER ONE

# Chalices of Prayer

When Padre Pio became a priest, his friends and family gave him a chalice. The chalice holds the wine that becomes the Precious Blood of Jesus. The chalice reminds us of Jesus' death. These chalices help us remember to pray for those who are suffering.

**DIRECTIONS**

- Cut out five chalices.
- Draw a picture of someone who is in pain on each chalice.
- Fill in the blank for each sentence "Jesus, heal the_____.
- In the blank, write the type of person the picture shows. For example: sad, lonely, broken arm of the boy, etc.
- Color the chalices.
- Glue the chalices on a large sheet of yellow paper.
- Take the chalices home and pray for these people.

### CENTER TWO

# Crosses of Suffering

The cross reminds us that Jesus suffered. Padre Pio did not like to see people suffer, so he built a hospital for them. Choose important words from Padre Pio's story and write them in the shape of a cross. This will help you remember the gifts that God gave to Padre Pio.

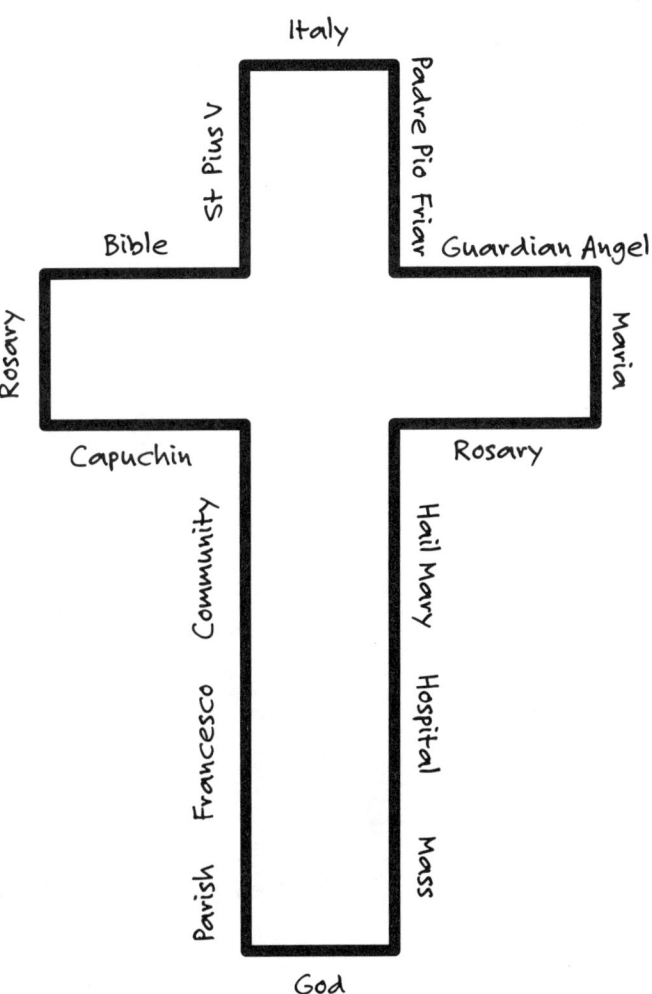

*Padre Pio* 95

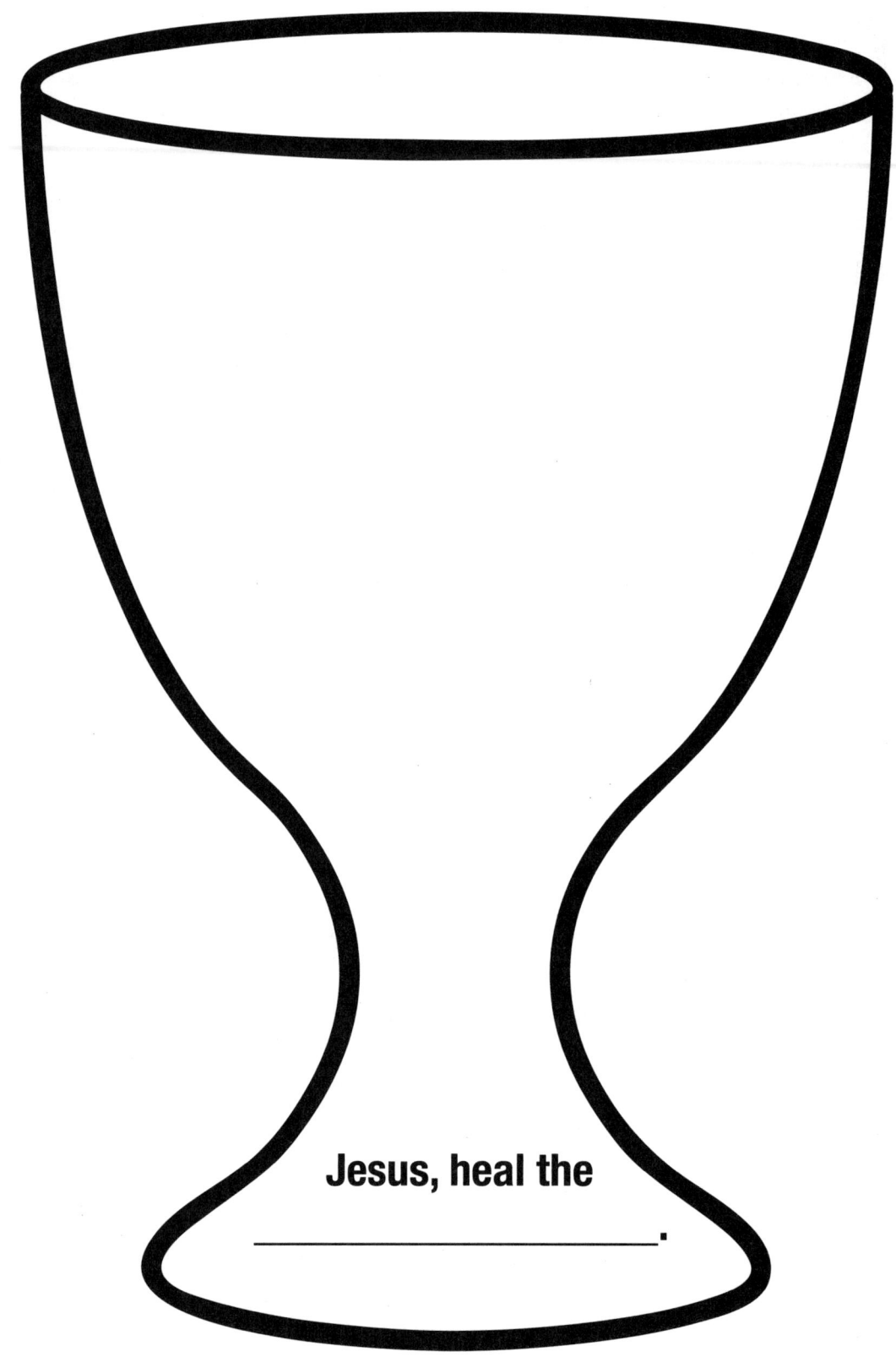

Jesus, heal the _____.

# CATECHIST PAGE FOR GRADES 4-6

## OBJECTIVES

- *To help children learn about Padre Pio by reading his story together*
- *At center one, students will review the traditional Mysteries of the Rosary and then write their own Mysteries of the Rosary*
- *At center 2, students will learn about cities in Italy and review facts about Padre Pio*

## MATERIALS

- *Hole punch*
- *Yarn*
- *One copy for each student of the map of Italy template found on page 101.*
- *Life Savers®: each student will need two, to glue on the map of Italy*
- *Pens for writing facts about Padre Pio on the map of Italy*
- *Angel, cross, flame and wine jar templates, 5 per each student, found on page 100.*

## Padre Pio's Story

**TEACHER:** On May 25, in 1887, Francesco Forgione was born. His older brother, Michele, was eager to have another member in the family so he had someone to play with. As the years passed, three more children were born—Felicita, Pellegrina, and Grazia.

**READER ONE:** The Forgione family were very devout Catholics. They went to Mass every day and prayed the Rosary together in the evenings. Following the Rosary, either the parents or grandparents told the children Bible stories. It was easy for their friends and neighbors to see that Christ was the center of their lives.

**READER TWO:** When Francesco grew older, after he received a lot of education, he entered the Capuchin order. He was called "Brother Pio." After more study, he was ordained a priest and then he was called "Padre Pio" (Padre means Father). As a priest he said Mass and taught children. Padre Pio also listened to people who had problems and helped them solve their problems.

**READER THREE:** Padre Pio did not like to see people suffer. He always wanted to heal them. He built a hospital to help the sick. The hospital had outstanding doctors and nurses who were well trained. God gave Padre Pio a very special gift. One day while he prayed, open sores suddenly appeared in the middle of the palms of his hands, on the bottoms of his feet, and in his side, which caused a lot of pain. These marks were like the wounds in Jesus' hands, feet, and side.

**READER FIVE:** When Padre Pio knew he was dying, he held a rosary in his hands. He said, "I see two mothers" (his own mother and Mary). A smile crossed his face and he died.

98 Learning Centers: Saints

## CENTER ONE: Personal Mysteries of the Rosary

There are four sets of mysteries we use when we pray the Rosary: The Joyful, the Luminous, the Sorrowful, and the Glorious. Each of us has times in our lives when we are joyous or sad, or when something great has happened to us or when we have been a light to others.

Using your life experiences, create your personal mysteries of the rosary. Here are some examples:

**JOYOUS MYSTERIES:** 1) My baby brother was born. 2) I made my First Communion. 3) I won the spelling bee. 4) I was confirmed. 5) I made a new friend.

**LUMINOUS MYSTERIES:** 1) I helped an elderly person cross the street. 2) I babysat for my younger brothers and sisters. 3) I played with someone that I usually don't play with. 4) I offered to take care of the recycling for my family. 5) I volunteered to serve Mass when it wasn't my turn.

**SORROWFUL MYSTERIES:** 1) My best friend moved away. 2) My dad got a new job, and we had to move to a new city. 3) My grandmother died. 4) My parents divorced. 5) I failed a test.

**GLORIOUS MYSTERIES:** 1) My team won regionals. 2) I lectored at Mass. 3) I passed a really hard test. 4) I was elected president of my class. 5) I was in my sister's wedding.

### DIRECTIONS

- Cut out five angels and write each of your personal Joyous Mysteries on an angel.
- Cut out five wine jars and write each of your personal Luminous Mysteries on a wine jar.
- Cut out five crosses and write each of your personal Sorrowful Mysteries on a cross.
- Cut out five flames of fire and write each of your personal Glorious Mysteries on a flame.
- Hole punch each one and put yarn through them and tie!

# Map of Italy and Facts about Padre Pio

Padre Pio was from Italy. Use the map of Italy. Glue a Life Saver® at the city where Padre Pio was born. Glue another Life Saver® at the city where he died. Write two facts about padre Pio on the map.

Padre Pio 101

# Saint Isaac Jogues

*Feastday: October 19*

---

CATECHIST'S PAGE FOR GRADES 1-3

---

### OBJECTIVES

■ *To help children understand the life of Father Isaac Jogues through reading "Saint Isaac's story"*

■ *At center one, to help children deepen their understanding of seeing, hearing, and feeling through creating sensory canoes*

■ *At center two, to help children know the names of the 12 apostles through creating apostle crowns*

### MATERIALS

■ *Three canoe templates, for each student found on page 103.*

■ *Markers, crayons, strips of paper, and apostle templates found on page 104.*

■ *Strips of paper for making a circle*

■ *12 apostle templates*

■ *Glue*

## Saint Isaac's Story

Can you imagine having enough children in your family to have your own baseball team? I was the fifth of nine children in my family. I attended school where the Jesuit brothers taught. I liked their kindness and their love for God, so I decided to become a Jesuit. I studied and became a priest and a missionary.

I took a very long boat trip with five Huron Native Americans. It was not a very comfortable trip; all we ate was boiled corn. We had to sleep out in the open, and the canoe was very crowded, so no one could stretch their legs. I did not speak the Huron language so the trip was very quiet.

I worked with the Native Americans; we built a mission center and I taught them about God. The Hurons liked me and the other priests who helped me.

One day, the Iroquois attacked some of the Hurons, the priests, and me. Everyone was taken prisoner. The Iroquois did not treat us well. They cut off our fingers and beat us with clubs. The Dutch men helped me get away. I went to Europe. My friends did not recognize me because I was so thin and my body had a lot of scars.

I missed my Native American friends and I wanted to help them live peacefully. I went back to try to help the Native Americans. The Iroquois still did not like me and my priest friends. One day, they killed all of us.

# Sensory Canoes

Students will have a deeper understanding of Saint Issac Jogues experiences by creating sensory canoes.

**DIRECTIONS**

- Cut out three canoes and decorate them.

- On one canoe, print "SEE."

- On the next canoe, print "HEAR."

- On the last canoe, print "FEEL".

- Read the biographical sketch; and put words or phrases that match each sense. For example: FEEL: sad, when fingers were cut off; pain, when the people were beaten with clubs; HEAR: silence as Father Isaac traveled; or running water as they canoed down the river.

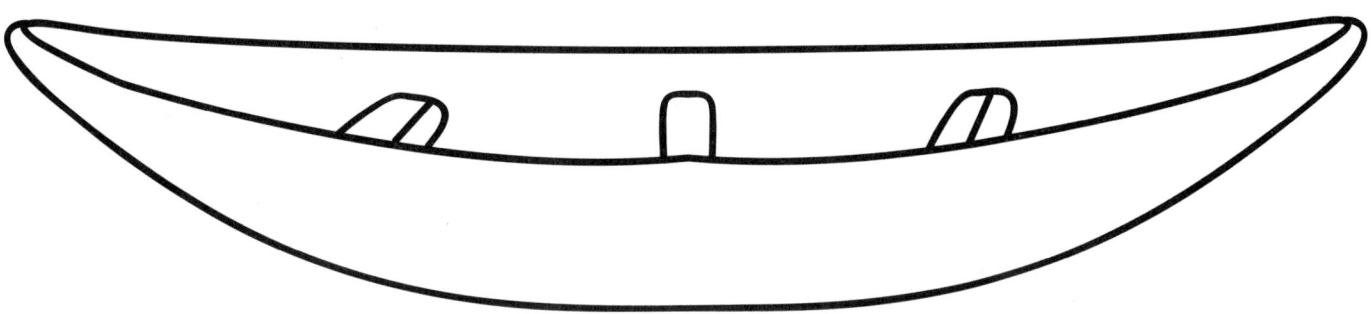

# Apostle Crowns

Saint Isaac Jogues studied about the apostles while learning to become a priest. Students will learn the apostles' names by making an apostle crown.

**DIRECTIONS**

- Take the strip of paper and glue the two ends together so it forms a circle that fits around your head.

- Cut out each apostle figure. Decorate it. Glue the apostles on the circle.

- You now, have an apostle crown. Remember, some of the apostles were martyrs just like Father Isaac and his friends.

*Isaac Jogues*

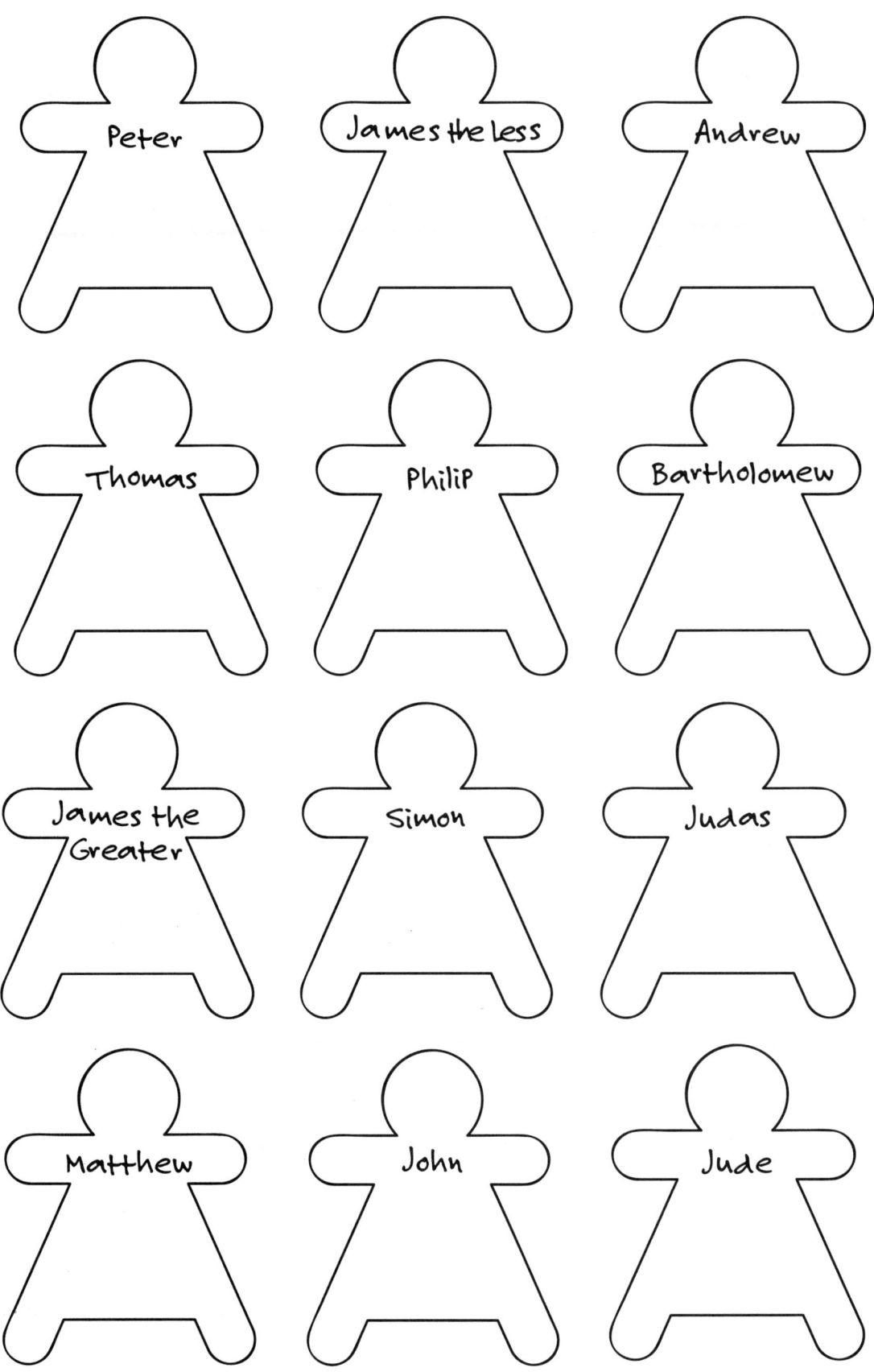

# CATECHIST'S PAGE FOR GRADES 4-6

### OBJECTIVES

- *To help children understand the life of Father Isaac Jogues through reading "Saint Isaac's story"*

- *Center one, to help children deepen their understanding of seeing, hearing, and feeling through creating sensory canoes and writing a story using these words*

- *Center two, to help children know the names of the 12 apostles and write one fact about each on one while creating an apostle crown*

### MATERIALS

- *Three canoe templates for each student, found on page 103.*

- *Markers, crayons for decorating canoe templates, strips of paper, and apostle templates found on page 104.*

- *Paper for writing a story about Father Isaac*

- *Glue*

## Saint Isaac's Story

**Teacher:** Isaac Jogues was born in 1607, and was the fifth of nine children. Just think, this family had their own baseball team! He attended a school where most of the teachers were Jesuit brothers. Isaac was so impressed with their kindness and their love for God, that he decided to become a Jesuit. Brother Isaac was ordained a priest and became a missionary.

**Reader One:** Father Isaac, along with five Huron Native Americans, began a long journey to the Huron reservation. This was a very difficult journey for Father Isaac. He didn't speak Huron, so there was a lot of silence as they traveled. The only food they ate was Indian corn. Everyone had to sleep out in the open. The canoe was very crowded, and there wasn't any room to stretch out.

**Reader Two:** Father Isaac worked with the Hurons and helped them build a mission center. He also taught them about God. The Hurons liked all the priests who worked with them.

**Reader Three:** Oh, no! An attack by the Iroquois! Most of the Hurons ran away, but some were killed and some were captured. Father Isaac and two other priests were captured. Unfortunately, the Iroquois began torturing these prisoners. The Iroquois cut off the prisoners' fingers and beat them with clubs. With the help of some neighboring Dutch people, Father Isaac escaped and returned to France.

**Reader Four:** His friends did not recognize him because he was so thin and his body had many scars on it. He wanted to return to the Hurons. Instead, he worked with the Iroquois trying to make a peace treaty. A few Hurons and Jean de Lalande traveled with him to meet with the Iroquois. When the Iroquois attacked them, the Hurons ran away, but de Lalande remained with Father Isaac. Both were killed.

**CENTER ONE**

# Sensory Canoes and Stories

Students will have a deeper understanding of Saint Issac Jogue's experiences through creating sensory canoes and writing their own stories.

## DIRECTIONS

■ Cut out three canoes and decorate them.

■ On one canoe, print "SEE."

■ On the next canoe, print "HEAR."

■ On the last canoe, print "FEEL".

■ Read the biographical sketch, and put words or phrases that match each word. For example: FEEL: sad, when fingers were cut off; pain, when the people were beat with clubs; HEAR: silence as Father Isaac traveled; water as they canoed down the river.

■ Write your own story about Father Isaac using the phrases on your canoes.

**CENTER TWO**

# Apostle Crowns and Facts

Saint Isaac Jogues studied about the apostles while learning to become a priest. Students will learn facts about the apostles through making the apostle crown.

## DIRECTIONS

■ Take the strip of paper and glue the two ends together so it forms a circle that fits around your head.

■ Cut out each apostle figure. Decorate it. Glue the apostles on the circle.

■ Write a fact about each apostle on the back side of each figure.

■ You now, have an apostle crown. Remember, some of the apostles were martyrs just like Father Isaac and his friends.

# Saint Frances Cabrini

*Feastday: November 13*

---

### CATECHIST'S PAGE GRADES 1-3

---

### OBJECTIVES

■ *To help children understand Mother Frances Cabrini through reading "Saint Frances Cabrini's story"*

■ *At center one, to help children review facts about Mother Cabrini through question/answer concentration circles*

■ *At center two, to help children become aware of hurts they have that need to be healed, and to become aware of people they trust through making a woven mat*

### MATERIALS

■ *Margarine lids or circles made from construction paper with questions and answers for concentration activity*

■ *Strips of paper for weaving a mat*

■ *Variety of colored construction paper for weaving*

■ *Markers for writing*

## Saint Frances Cabrini's Story

Can you imagine what it would be like to have 12 brothers and sisters? I was the youngest of thirteen children. I was weak when I was born, so my parents took me to be baptized immediately.

My father often read stories about missionaries to us. As I played, I pretended my dolls were missionaries. I dreamed of becoming a missionary.

When I was thirteen, I attended a private school. After I graduated, I tried to become a sister in hopes I would eventually go to China. Because I was not well, the sisters told me "no."

Smallpox broke out in the village and my parents died. Soon I caught the disease. My sister Rosa nursed me until I was well.

I was hired to take care of orphans. Six other women helped me run the orphanage. These women and I began a new religious order. We became the Missionary Sisters of the Sacred Heart of Jesus.

Our religious community traveled to the United States. A very generous lady bought us a home, and we opened an orphanage. We also opened schools and a hospital.

The sisters and I were preparing for a Christmas party. I was putting candy in little bags for the children, when I had a heart attack and died. I was the first American citizen to be made a saint.

---

*Saint Frances Cabrini* 107

# Question/Answer Concentration Circles

**CENTER ONE**

Students will learn basic facts about Saint Cabrini by playing this comprehension game. Give each child 10 margarine lids or paper circles. Five lids or paper circles will have questions on one side and five lids or paper circles will have answers on the other side.

Place the questions and answer lids face down in rows. Play concentration, taking turns turning over the circles until the correct question and answer are found.

**HERE ARE SOME QUESTIONS AND ANSWERS:**

| Questions | Answers |
|---|---|
| How many children were in Mother Cabrini's family? | 13 |
| Where did Frances live when she was little? | on a farm |
| Who read to Frances and her brothers and sisters? | Her dad |
| Who took care of Frances when she was small? | Rosa |
| What did Frances study to be? | Teacher |
| When Frances played with dolls, what did she pretend the flowers were? | Missionaries |
| What disease killed her parents? | Smallpox |
| What killed Mother Cabrini? | Heart Attack |

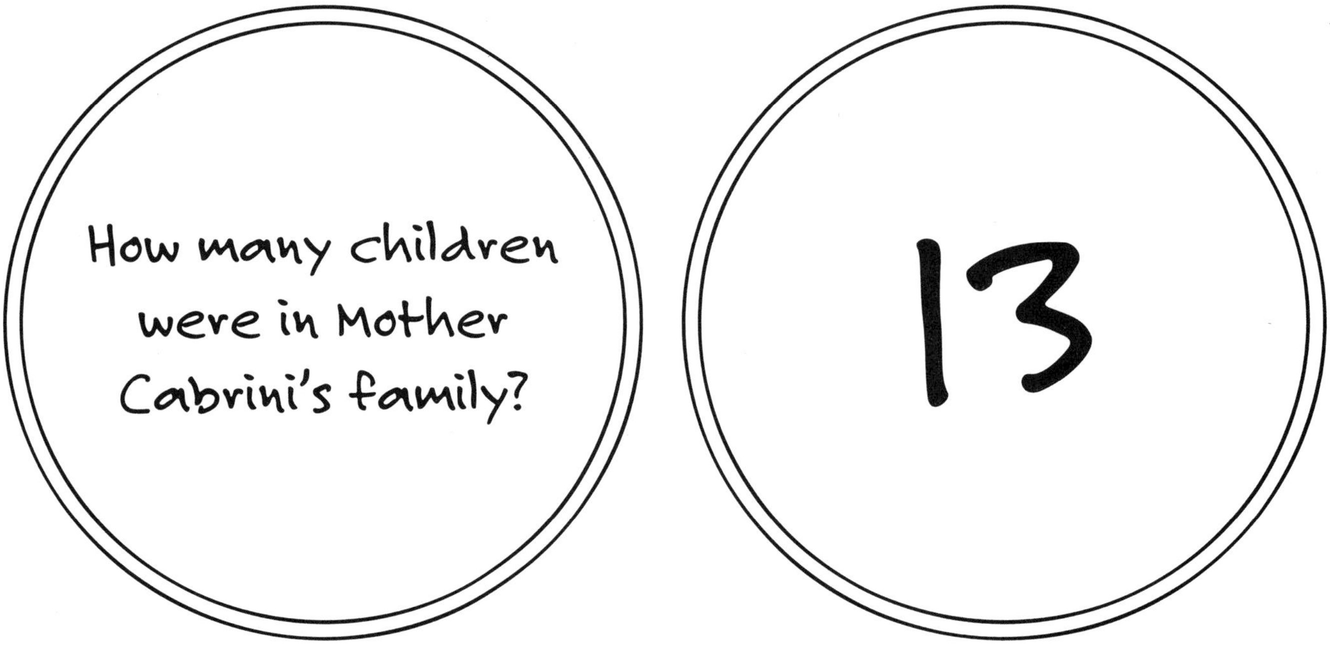

( How many children were in Mother Cabrini's family? )   ( 13 )

108 Learning Centers: Saints

# Healing Mat

**CENTER TWO**

Frances' father read Bible stories to the children. Her favorite story was the healing of the paralyzed man (Mark 2:1-12). Creating a healing mat reminds students to pray for those who need healing and to ask for the healing they need.

**DIRECTIONS**

■ Read the Bible story with a friend. After reading the story, weave a mat following the directions below.

■ After making the mat, think about which friends or family members you would ask to take you to Jesus if you needed healing. Print names on one side of the mat.

■ On the other side of the mat, write a prayer asking Jesus to heal one of your hurts. For example: "Jesus, please heal me so I will not fight with my brother," or "Jesus, please heal me so that I will do what my parents ask."

■ Take two sheets of paper, in your choice of colors. Cut one sheet into nine strips that are 1 inch wide and 12 inches long. Take the other sheet and cut it into 12 strips that are 1 inch wide and 9 inches long.

■ Place the long, 12-inch strips horizontally, and weave the short strips vertically.

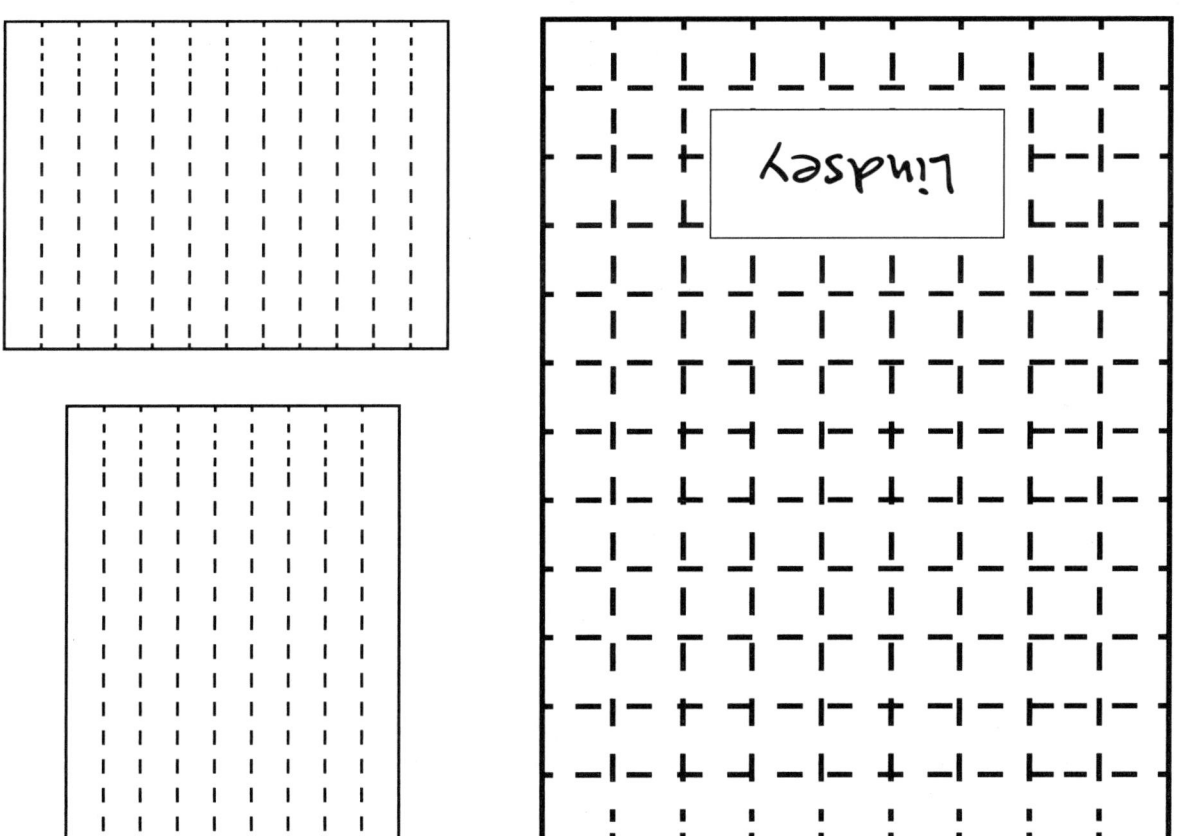

*Saint Frances Cabrini* 109

# CATECHIST'S PAGE GRADES 4-6

## OBJECTIVES

- *To help children understand Mother Frances Cabrini through reading "Saint Frances Cabrini's Story"*

- *At center one, help children focus on sounds found in the "Saint Frances Cabrini's Story" through writing a sound poem*

- *At center two, to help children become aware of weaknesses they have that need to be healed and to become aware of people they trust through making a woven mat.*

## MATERIALS

- *Paper for writing a sound poem*
- *Strips of paper for weaving a mat*
- *Variety of colored construction paper for weaving*
- *Markers for writing*
- *Ear Template found on page 111.*

## Saint Frances Cabrini's Story

**READER ONE:** Can you imagine what it would be like to have 12 brothers and sisters? Frances Cabrini was the youngest of thirteen children. She was very weak when she was born, so her parents took her to the church to be baptized immediately.

**READER TWO:** Frances's father often read to the children in the evening. He read about missionaries. As Frances played, she loved to pretend that her dolls were missionaries. She also sailed paper boats filled with flowers. In her imagination, the flowers were missionaries who taught in China. At a very young age, Frances dreamed of becoming a missionary.

**READER THREE:** When she was thirteen, she attended a private school. After she graduated, she tried to become a sister in hopes that she would eventually go to China. Because she was not well, the sisters told her no. Smallpox broke out in the village; her parents died. Frances caught the disease. Her sister Rosa nursed her, and Frances recuperated.

**READER FOUR:** Frances was hired to run an orphanage. She spent time in prayer. Six other women joined her and helped her run the orphanage. Frances and these women founded a new religious order and became the Missionary Sisters of the Sacred Heart of Jesus.

**READER FIVE:** Frances and her religious sisters went to the United States. When they arrived, there was no house for them to live in. A very generous lady bought them a home, and they opened an orphanage. As the years went by, they opened schools and hospitals.

**READER SIX:** Mother Cabrini and her sisters were preparing for a Christmas party. She was putting candy in little bags for the children when she had a heart attack and died. Mother Cabrini was the first American citizen to be made a saint.

**CENTER ONE**

# Sound Poem

Saint Francis Cabrini often listened to others. Sounds are all around us. It is important to recognize when we need to listen and when we need to tune sounds out. The ear helps student focus on sounds.

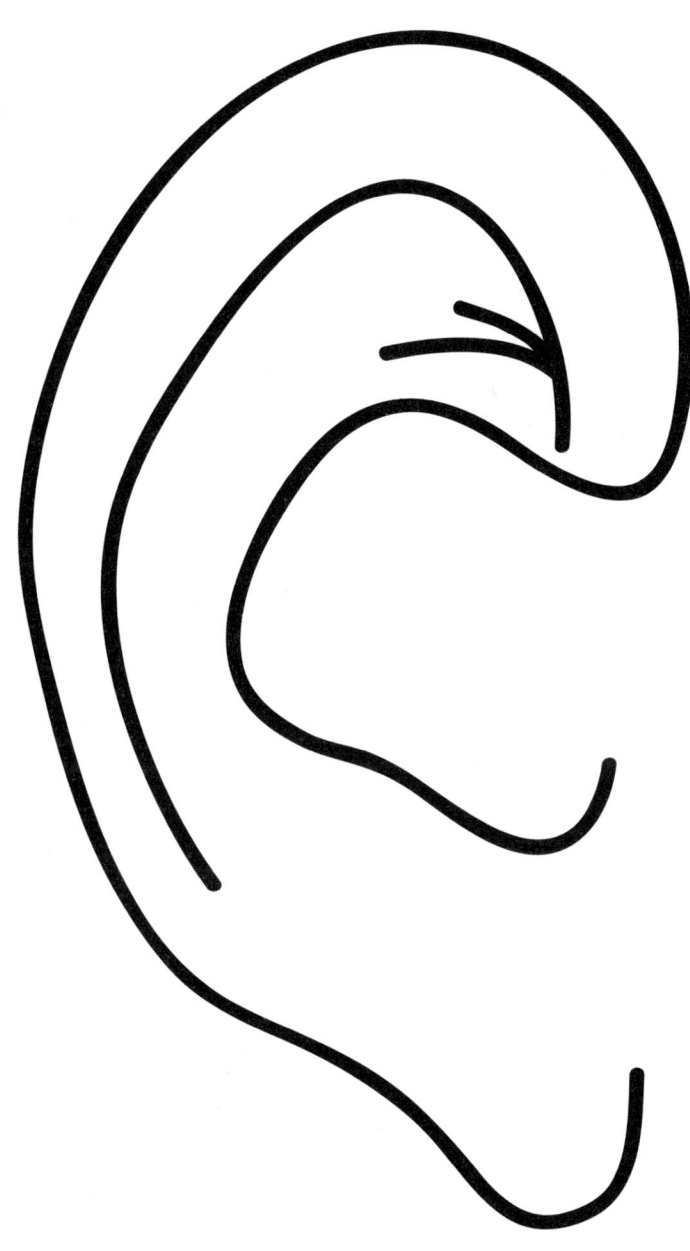

**DIRECTIONS**

- Cut out the ear template and color it.

- On a piece of paper write a six-line sound poem using sounds found within the biographical sketch.

- Write the poem on the ear template.

- Share it with a friend

Here is an example:
*Sounds of Mother Cabrini*
*Babies cry*
*Goats bleat*
*Rivers roar*
*People moan*
*Children laugh*
*Mother Cabrini cries*

*Saint Frances Cabrini*

## CENTER TWO: Healing Mat

Saint Frances's father read Bible stories to the children. One of Saint Cabrini's favorite stories was the healing of the paralyzed man (Mark 2:1-12). Creating a healing mat reminds students to pray for those who need healing and to ask for the healing they need.

**DIRECTIONS**

■ Read the story with a friend. After reading the story, weave a mat following the directions below.

■ After making the mat, think about which friends you would ask to take you to Jesus if you needed healing. Print your friends' names on one side of the mat.

■ On the other side of the mat, write a sentence asking Jesus to heal one of your weaknesses. For example, "Jesus, please heal me so I will not fight with my brother," or "Jesus, heal me so that I will obey my parents."

■ Take two sheets of paper, in your choice of colors. Cut one sheet into nine strips that are 1 inch wide and 12 inches long. Take the other sheet and cut it into 12 strips that are 1 inch wide and 9 inches long.

■ Place the long, 12 inch strips horizontally and weave the short strips vertically.

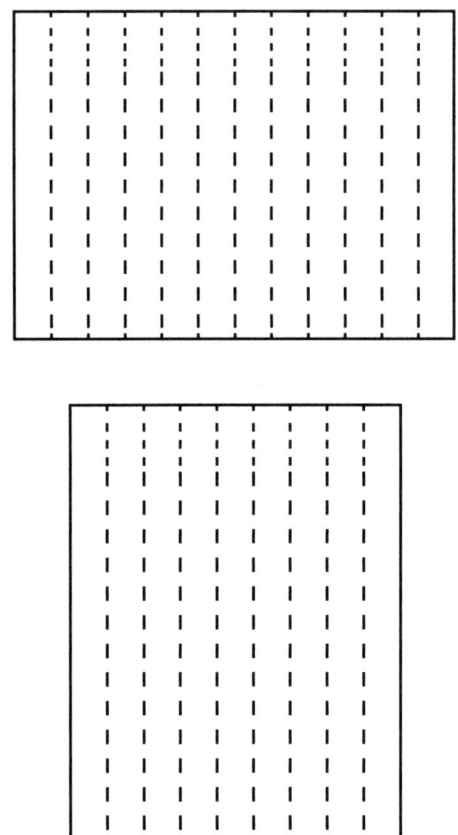

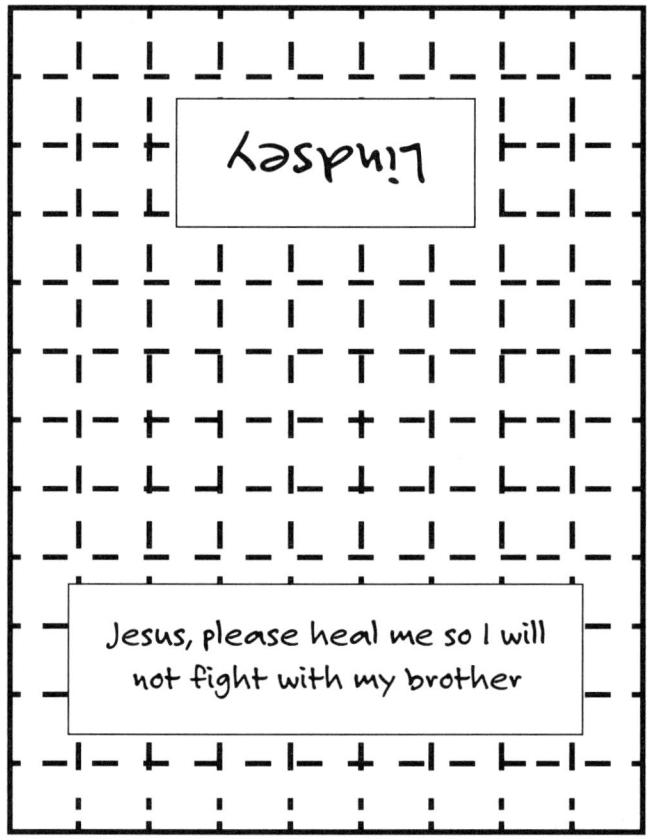

112 Learning Centers: Saints

# Saint Rose Philippine Duchesne

*Feastday:* November 18

## CATECHIST'S PAGE FOR GRADES 1-3

**OBJECTIVES**

■ To help children learn about St. Rose Philippine through reading "St. Rose Philippine's Story"

■ At center one, help children create a hand wreath as a reminder to pray always

■ At center two, help them make Rose Flowers to remember Rose's life

**MATERIALS**

■ Different colors of construction paper so each student can trace his/her hand ten times

■ Markers to write on the hands

■ Glue

■ Flower template

■ Crayons, markers

## Saint Rose Philippine's Story

Long ago, a little girl was born in a small town in southern France called Grenoble. Her parents named her Rose-Philippine. When Rose was seven, she went to school, where she learned to read and write. It was there that she decided to become a religious sister and dreamed of being a missionary.

When Rose grew up, she became a sister. She prayed a lot and taught school. Rose was happy, but she dreamed of a time when she could go to America and work with the Native Americans, then called Indians.

One day, Rose and several other sisters got on a ship and sailed to America. Rose got so sick on the ship that she almost died. When she got well, all of the sisters took another boat ride to St. Charles, Missouri, where they lived in a log cabin. It was very cold there, and the sisters couldn't speak English very well.

Soon the sisters opened a school for girls. Rose liked this very much, but she still wanted to help the Indian people. Finally, when Rose was 72, she worked at an Indian school in Kansas. Rose prayed for the people there day and night. Soon the Indians nicknamed her "Quahkahkanumad," which means "Woman Who Prays Always."

Rose only stayed at the Indian school one year and then returned to St. Charles because she became ill. Rose's dream came true. She was a missionary. Rose lived until she was 83 years old.

*Saint Rose Philippine Duchesne*

**CENTER ONE**

# Pray Always Wreath

The Native Americans nicknamed St. Rose "Quahkahkanumad," which means "Woman Who Prays Always." The wreath will remind students to pray always. When you pray often, you are being like St. Rose-Philippine.

**DIRECTIONS**

■ Have children trace one of their hands 10 times.

■ Cut out hands.

■ On seven of the hands write the names of people students want to pray for.

■ On the other three hands have students write the name of three favorite prayers.

■ Glue in the shape of a wreath with wrists overlapping a little. Then decorate.

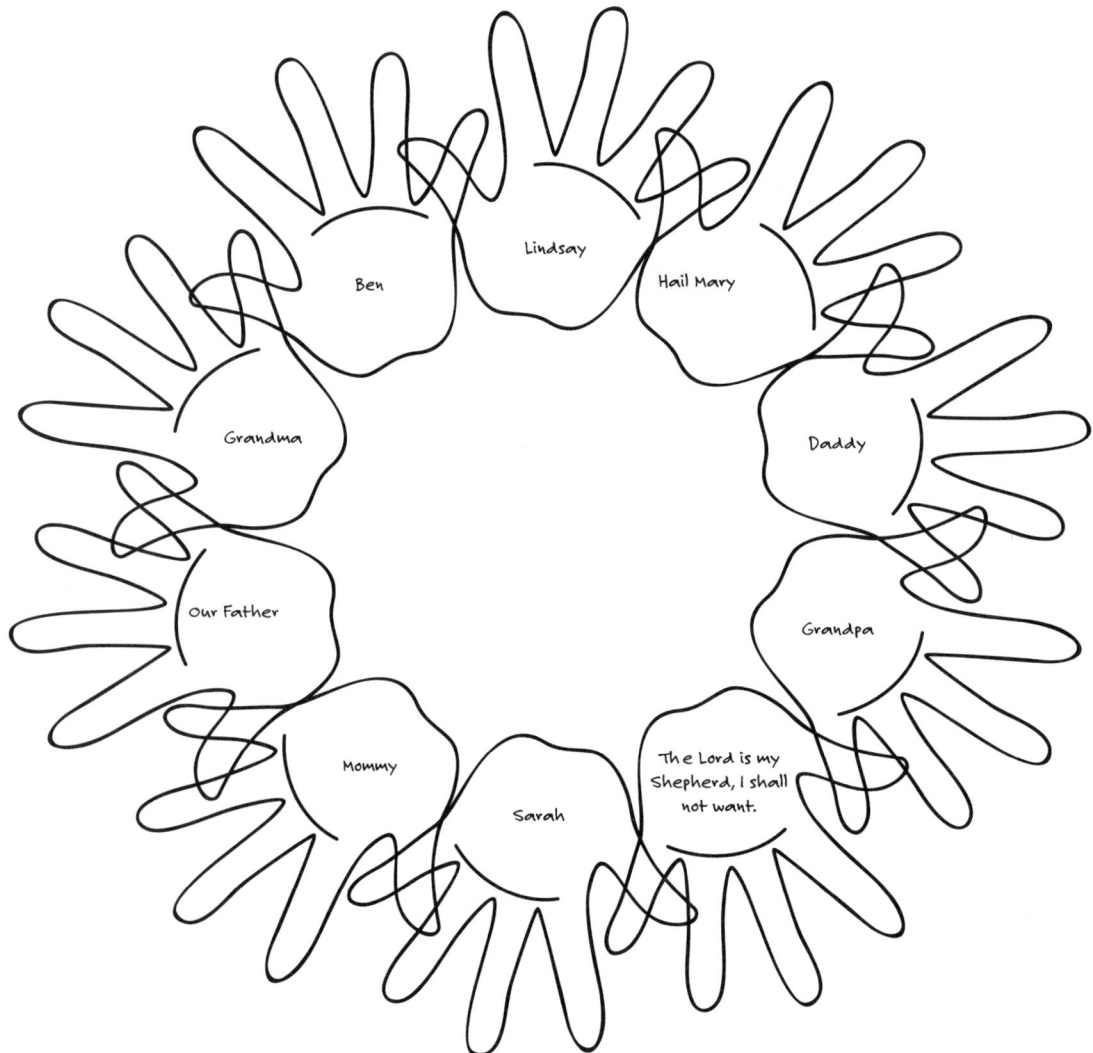

114 Learning Centers: Saints

# Remembering Rose Flowers

St. Rose's name reminds us of a flower. Students will remember important facts about St. Rose by creating simple flowers.

**DIRECTIONS**

- Cut out the flower center.
- Cut out 8 petals.
- On each petal, draw a picture about Rose or write a word describing her.
- Decorate the center and the petals.
- Glue flower petals onto center.
- Glue flower onto a straw.

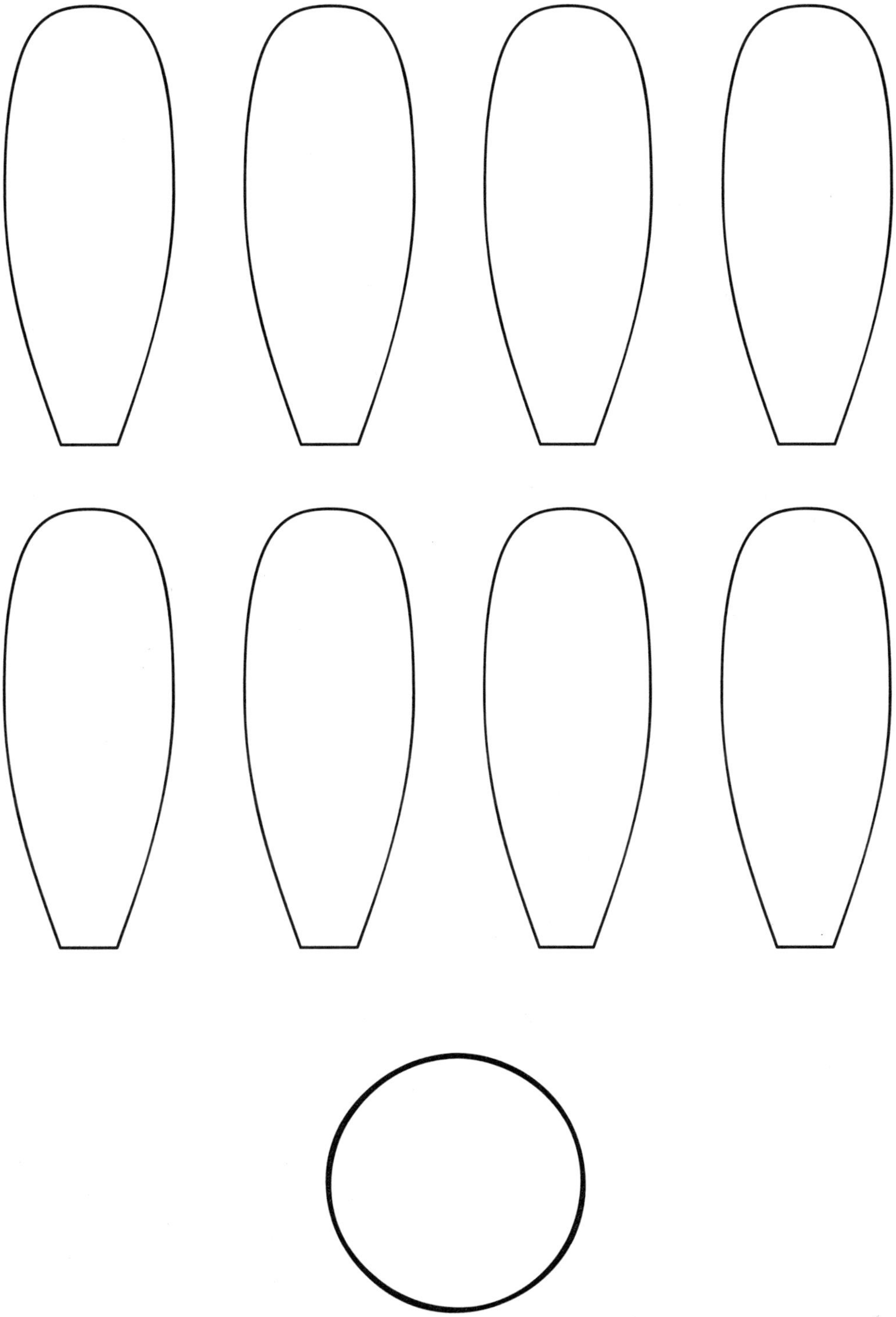

*Saint Rose Philippine Duchesne* 115

# CATECHIST PAGE FOR GRADES 4-6

## OBJECTIVES

- To help children learn about the life about Saint Rose Pilippine by reading "Saint Rose Pilippine's Story"

- At center one, to help children gain a deeper knowledge of themselves through writing and sharing a bio poem

- At center two, to help children remember important facts about Rose's life through working on a comment card

## MATERIALS

- Scrap paper for writing bio poems

- Variety of colored construction paper for final draft of bio poems

- Markers for writing final draft of bio poem

- Copies of the six-box comment cards, one for each student, found on page 119.

## St. Rose Philippine's Story

**TEACHER:** In 1769, a special little girl was born who was baptized in St. Louis Church in Grenoble, France. She received the name "Rose" in honor of St. Rose of Lima. Her middle name "Philippine" came from the apostle Philip's name.

**READER ONE:** Rose went to the Convent of the Visitation School, where she learned to read and write. When Rose was eight, she heard a Jesuit missionary speak about his work in the Americas, and dreamed of becoming a sister and a missionary.

**READER TWO:** At age 18, Rose joined the Visitations. A terrible war broke out and all the sisters had to leave the convent. After the war, Rose and a few other sisters joined The Society of the Sacred Heart. All of the sisters spent time praying and teaching.

**READER THREE:** Finally, in 1818, Rose's dream came true. She and four other religious sisters boarded a ship in France and set sail to America. While Rose was on the ship, she became very ill and almost died. The sisters who were with Rose were very scared. When they landed in America, they decided to stay in Louisiana for a while until Rose was better. When Rose was well, the sisters boarded a smaller boat and went up the Mississippi River to St. Charles, Missouri. Life there was very hard for the sisters: they were poor, it was very cold, and they had a hard time learning English.

**READER FOUR:** Even with these difficulties, the sisters opened a school for girls. Rose enjoyed teaching the girls, but she still dreamed of teaching Native Americans. When Rose was 72, a school was built in Kansas for the children of the Potawatomi Tribe. Rose went to Kansas and was nicknamed "Quahkahkanumad," which means "Woman Who Prays Always." Rose only stayed there one year and then returned to St. Charles because she got sick. Her dream had come true; she was a missionary. She died at the age of 83.

# Bio Poem

**CENTER ONE**

Saint Rose Philippine was a very gifted person. She wrote a poem about herself. Students will recognize their own gifts and talents by writing a bio poem about themselves.

**DIRECTIONS**

■ A bio poem is a poem that describes a person in 11 lines. There is a specific formula to use when writing a bio poem.

■ Write a bio poem about yourself.

■ Share your poem with your classmates.

**FORMULA**

■ First name

■ Four adjectives that describe the person

■ Son or daughter of (your parents names)

■ Lover of (three different things that the person loves)

■ Who feels (three different feelings and when or where they are felt)

■ Who gives (three different things the person gives)

■ Who fears (three different fears the person has)

■ Who would like to see (three different things the person would like to see)

■ Who lives (a brief description of where the person lives)

■ Last name

Let's imagine that Rose wrote the following bio poem:

## ROSE

*Courageous, thoughtful, kind, prayerful*
*Daughter of Mr. and Mrs. Duchesne*
*Lover of the sick, the poor, and the Native Americans*
*Who feels sad when the war broke out and she had to leave the convent; who feels happy that she was able to go to the United States; who feels disappointed that she could only live with the Native Americans for one year*
*Who gives service, happiness, and encouragement*
*Who fears the war, the long ocean journey, and not speaking English well*
*Who would like to see more schools opened, more time spent with the Native Americans, and better health for her sisters and herself*
*Who lives in a log cabin in the United States*
*Duchesne*

# Comment Cards

Students will remember important facts about Saint Rose Philippine by filling out comment cards.

**DIRECTIONS**

■ After reading the biographical sketch about Saint Rose Philippine, complete a six-box comment card.

■ Glue the comment box on a piece of plain paper and draw a picture of Saint Rose Philippine. Title your paper "Saint Rose Philippine."

■ Share your answers with your classmates.

| | |
|---|---|
| My favorite part was: | One idea that surprised me was: |
| One question I would ask Rose is: | I believe: |
| I did not like: | I wonder: |

Saint Rose Philippine Duchesne

# OF RELATED INTEREST

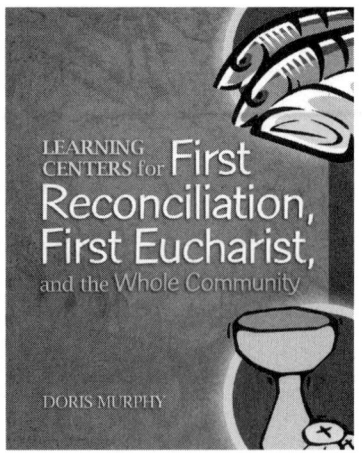  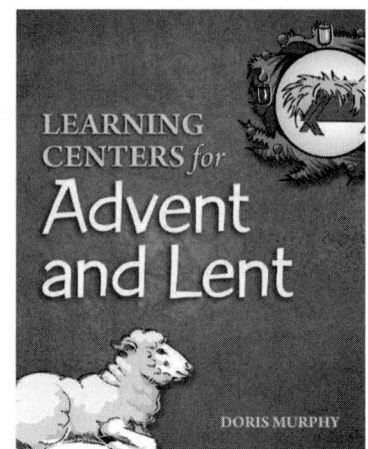

### LEARNING CENTERS FOR FIRST RECONCILIATION, FIRST EUCHARIST, and the Whole Community
DORIS MURPHY

Included are 37 creative and formative centers for children preparing for first reconciliation and first Eucharist. Also included are eight "gatherings" for the whole community to help children experience the learning centers with the support of the wider parish family.

**96 pages | $16.95 | 978-1-58595-564-7**

### LEARNING CENTERS FOR CONFIRMATION
DORIS MURPHY

Here are 15 creative and formative centers to help young people and their families share church teaching, Scripture, prayers, conversations, and fun activities that reinforces the teaching.

**80 pages | $16.95 | 978-1-58595-757-6**

### LEARNING CENTERS FOR ADVENT AND LENT
DORIS MURPHY

Everything you need—including reproducibles—to create 30 fun creative learning centers for Advent, Lent, and Holy Week (plus 9 "seasonal centers") to help parents share the faith with their children.

**120 pages | $16.95 | 978-1-58595-686-9**

### 70 SACRAMENT STARTERS FOR CHILDREN
...and those who teach them
PATRICIA MATHSON

These simple, beautiful, and indispensable activities offer ten creative ways to celebrate and learn about each of the seven sacraments.

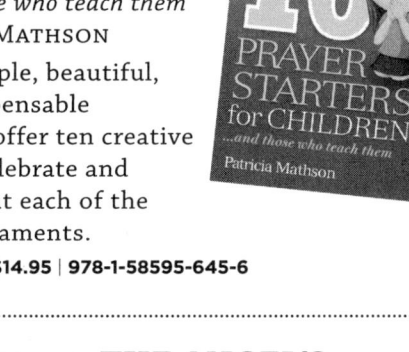

**104 pages | $14.95 | 978-1-58595-645-6**

### THE ANGEL'S SACRAMENT LESSON (DVD)

This delightful video covers all seven sacraments and gives children background information as well as the theology of the sacraments. For ages 7-10.

**11 minutes | $19.95**
**978-1-58595-730-9**

**1-800-321-0411**
WWW.23RDPUBLICATIONS.COM